ETHNOPOLITICS IN ECUADOR:
INDIGENOUS RIGHTS AND THE
STRENGTHENING OF DEMOCRACY

Ethnopolitics in Ecuador:
Indigenous Rights and the Strengthening of Democracy

BY MELINA SELVERSTON-SCHER
with a Foreword by Luis Macas

The publisher of this book is the North-South Center Press at the University of Miami.

The mission of The Dante B. Fascell North-South Center is to promote better relations and serve as a catalyst for change among the United States, Canada, and the nations of Latin America and the Caribbean by advancing knowledge and understanding of the major political, social, economic, and cultural issues affecting the nations and peoples of the Western Hemisphere.

Cover photo © by Kari Lu Gilmore, of indigenous protestors observing negotiations in the national palace in Quito: Agrarian law protests, 1994. All photographs in the text © copyright Kari Lu Gilmore.

Library of Congress Cataloging-in-Publication Data

Selverston-Scher, Melina.
Ethnopolitics in Ecuador: Indigenous Rights and the Strengthening of Democracy.
p. cm.
ISBN 1-57454-090-4 (hc:alk.paper) — ISBN 1-57454-091-2 (pb:alk.paper)

Printed in the United States of America/TS
∞ The paper used in this publication meets the requirements of the American National Standards for Information Sciences — Permanence of Paper for Printed Library Materials, ANSI Z39.48.1984.

05 04 03 02 01   6 5 4 3 2 1

Contents

Prólogo

LUIS MACAS

ANTECEDENTES

Uno de los valores profundos que los pueblos indígenas ostentan hasta el día de hoy, sin duda alguna, es su capacidad de resistencia frente a las adversidades de la colonización europea: su fortaleza ante la explotación económica, la opresión política, el estado de exclusión, y la discriminación social que forman parte de ese legado colonial. Dentro de nuestros pueblos, perviven valores, conocimientos, sabidurías, pero sobre todo, aún están vigentes instituciones culturales, económicas y políticas propias, a pesar de todas las adversidades.

Son éstos los principios y el contenido que fluyen en el interior de los pueblos y comunidades indígenas y que principalmente determinan las luchas, las propuestas y los logros del movimiento indígena contemporáneo. Si describimos estas instituciones diversas que han permitido la organización, las relaciones sociales, la espiritualidad indígena y las relaciones con la madre naturaleza, decimos que son, entre otras: el *ayllu* (familia), *ayllu llakta* (comuna), *minka* (trabajo colectivo), *rimanakuy* (el diálogo), *yuyarinakuy* (acuerdos), y el *pacha mama* (naturaleza). En fin, éstos son los referentes de vida de las comunidades y, por tanto, de lucha por su mantenimiento y perfeccionamiento en la época contemporánea.

Si bien estas instituciones fueron los soportes en la construcción de las sociedades de los pueblos indígenas, también hoy en día figuran como postulados en la propuesta indígena hacia cambios profundos de la sociedad, en procura de construir un Estado con verdadera identidad nacional. Pero el proceso del movimiento indígena ha sido capaz de percibir en sus propuestas otra dimensión compleja, basada en las experiencias de convivencia con la sociedad dominante, que es la de asumir una posición como conciencia y

---

El doctor Luis Macas, antiguo Presidente de la Confederación de las Nacionalidades Indígenas del Ecuador (CONAIE), es en la actualidad Rector de la Universidad Intercultural de las Nacionalidades y Pueblos Indígenas del Ecuador y Director del Instituto Científico de Culturas Indígenas del Ecuador (ICCI).

lucha de clase. Pues, desde esta perspectiva, desde esta conciencia social, se ha instrumentado un conjunto de herramientas de lucha, hacia la superación de los complejos problemas de la sociedad en su conjunto. Estas herramientas son, la concepción del Estado, sus estructuras, el sistema político, la restringida situación de la democracia, la inequidad y la injusticia, entre otras.

Dos líneas de acción

Éstos son algunos de los temas que podemos señalar como referentes de lucha durante el proceso de desarrollo organizativo del movimiento indígena. Sin embargo, desde esta visión y estas experiencias, nuestras organizaciones establecen dos dimensiones importantes en su estrategia de lucha y que constituyen dos líneas fundamentales de acción:

- Una línea de acción se identifica en el marco de la dimensión histórico-cultural — étnica — cuyo significado se expresa en la lucha por las demandas de reivindicación indígenas y de soluciones inmediatas, que necesariamente formarán el contenido fundamental de una agenda de planteamientos de carácter endógeno de los pueblos y comunidades indígenas. Es decir, las luchas en esta dirección son en sí generadas desde los intereses de las nacionalidades y pueblos, que son derechos legítimos e históricos que no han sido ejercidos con el reconocimiento del Estado y la sociedad dominante. Sin embargo, estas demandas nacen desde el interior de dichos sectores. Para algunos tratadistas, esta dimensión representa un fenómeno de carácter exclusivamente étnico, antropológico, donde se esgrime y se principaliza un enfoque etnocentrista o el indigenismo excluyente.

- Otra concepción o línea de acción que está presente en la estrategia del movimiento indígena ecuatoriano hace relación a la dimensión social, a la lucha desde la conciencia de clase a partir de su identidad en el contexto de la sociedad contemporánea. Esta línea de acción incluye las concepciones y prácticas que los pueblos indígenas adoptaron desde una comprensión vivencial de los fenómenos sociales y políticos y de los problemas del mundo que nos rodea.

La comprensión de esta dimensión y su práctica en las acciones han sido una constante en la línea de conducción del movimiento indígena a lo largo de su proceso de organización y construcción ideológica. Sin duda, esta orientación constituye un referente fundamental en la estrategia indígena, que es su conciencia social de clase, por lo que el movimiento indígena se convierte en catalizador y sintetizador de las diversas demandas sectoriales, y es, ante todo, el sujeto social que centraliza la demanda y lucha por un interés colectivo y global. Por tanto, esta comprensión es lo que articula lo étnico-cultural y la lucha social de clase del movimiento indígena del Ecuador.

Como es evidente, los planteamientos y acciones indígenas se orientan en el marco de las dos dimensiones o concepciones de lucha. Una primera línea se dirige hacia lo reivindicativo, lo cultural y basado en aspiraciones inmediatas — o sea, hacia lo entendido también como intereses concretos y sectoriales, en este caso desde la perspectiva de las nacionalidades, los pueblos y las comunidades. Sin embargo, la visión de lo reivindicativo, de lo inmediato y concreto no es exclusivo ni excluyente; se establece otra línea de acción, con orientaciones más amplias desde una comprensión de la lucha global, en una realidad social, económica, cultural y política actuales. Las luchas emprendidas desde el movimiento indígena se inscriben en un contexto de la problemática general. Es decir, sus acciones se han identificado siempre con las demandas de otros sectores sociales y sobre la unidad de los objetivos comunes en la construcción de un Estado nuevo y una sociedad distinta.

La lucha indígena y su propuesta

Sólo a partir del entendimiento y ejercicio de las dos dimensiones — la visión histórico-cultural y la posición y conciencia de clase — surge la propuesta indígena perfectible y coherente; ubicando la acción social y política desde el cuestionamiento a las estructuras del Estado y a un sistema social, económico y político inadecuado y obsoleto, que no se compadece con la realidad actual. Bajo estas consideraciones, la iniciativa del movimiento indígena involucra a toda la sociedad en sus demandas y perspectivas. De hecho, algunos puntos de la agenda que advierten aceptación y consensos se pueden señalar de la siguiente manera: instaurar la práctica del diálogo hacia la consecución de los consensos, efectuar la construcción de un Estado Plurinacional, realizar un reencuentro en la interculturalidad y la diversidad social y cultural, y lograr la ampliación y profundización de la democracia, la equidad y la justicia social.

Las diversas formas de lucha dadas a lo largo de la historia colonial y republicana del Ecuador, es necesario precisarlo, fueron respuestas a las condiciones de postergación de nuestros pueblos, y podemos identificar dichas luchas con los grandiosos levantamientos de Tupak Amaru, Fernando Daquilema, y otros, hasta que la conciencia indígena desemboca en las acciones de la década de los 90, en función de instituir en el país modificaciones estructurales e históricas como la visibilización del movimiento indígena en el Estado y la sociedad, y el reconocimiento institucional de la diversidad de identidades, su dignidad y sus derechos.

Al hacer una descripción sobre la evolución y los avances de los pueblos indígenas, nos atrevemos a mencionar que los varios *ejes* fundamentales que articularon el proceso indígena, durante la instrumentación y estructuración de las organizaciones modernas del movimiento, se pueden resumir en una sola palabra: *dignidad* – es decir, la lucha por el derecho a la tierra y territorios y por el fortalecimiento de la identidad, como son el reconocimiento de las lenguas y la educación indígena, entre otros objetivos, se inscriben en este marco de convergencia.

Estos principios de lucha se convierten en los contenidos determinantes durante las décadas de los 50 y 60, época que se caracteriza por la euforia de la comunalización de nuestros pueblos, bajo la aplicación de una legislación intencionada unilateralmente desde el Estado. Además, en ese momento por una parte se institucionaliza el *ayllu llakta*, o comuna, y, por otra, la acción del control directo y vertical del Estado, control que representa, en nuestro conocimiento, la imposición de una institución ajena en un franco debilitamiento de la institucionalidad milenaria. Durante esa misma época también surgen en el Ecuador las organizaciones comunales, o se constituye la organización de primer grado, como se denomina ésta en la actualidad dentro de los niveles de organización que practican nuestros pueblos. Por supuesto, la organización comunal o de primer grado es la organización nuclear, primigenia, después de la familia – una institución original de los pueblos indígenas y con un concepto absolutamente distinto de lo que es la organización de los pueblos.

Esta institución, el *ayllu llakta*, afectó mayoritariamente a los pueblos indígenas, pero también a los sectores campesinos y afroecuatorianos. Sin embargo, la adopción tardía de la institución comunal se explica por los años que habían transcurrido desde la expedición de la Ley de Comunas en 1936 y debido a que la estrategia de aplicación estatal de dicha ley tenía sus falencias. Esta anomalía institucional requería un diseño propio basado en los intereses de los pueblos indígenas, y ahí es cuando el proceso indígena rebasa la oferta del Estado, al procurar ampliar y reforzar el curso del desarrollo organizacional estructurando las organizaciones de segundo y tercer grado y planteando estas estructuras como contenido principal de la estrategia indígena.

Es importante subrayar esta etapa de organización y lucha en el contexto de la unidad indígena, porque esta lucha necesariamente tiene como base el reconocimiento de las tierras ancestrales y comunales. Es decir, al convalidar el Estado la ley de comunas, los pueblos indígenas consolidan la unidad que servirá de base o *eje* para conseguir otra conquista: la Ley de Reforma Agraria, cuya expedición se da en 1964. Ya en esta línea de confrontación con el Estado actúa la constante o temática actual que es el problema histórico de la tenencia de *tierras*.

Como se hizo evidente durante la lucha de la década de los 70, cuando se forjan y se articulan las organizaciones de tercer grado y se advierte la presencia de las organizaciones regionales, el motivo central de la dinámica indígena es la recuperación de las tierras en la región andina y la defensa de los territorios en la región amazónica y la Costa. La lucha por los derechos territoriales se ejercen desde las organizaciones provinciales y una organización regional en los Andes del Ecuador, el Ecuador Runacunapac Riccharimui (ECUARUNARI), donde se implementan líneas de acción hacia la consecución de una verdadera unidad de los pueblos, contextos que generan otros frentes de lucha como el planteamiento de la atención a la educación, la salud y otros servicios.

Una de las épocas más importantes desde la experiencia de los pueblos indígenas sin duda es la década de los 80, cuando se produce una dinámica cualitativamente muy importante. Se diría que es el reencuentro de las nacionalidades y pueblos. Es cuando se inicia un debate amplio y sostenido, tanto en su contenido como en la obertura. Es cuando los pueblos indígenas vierten los insumos para una elaboración posterior de la estrategia indígena. Es el asumir y el ejercicio por parte de los pueblos indígenas de una dimensión de conciencia social como entidad cultural y como clase. Y el evento de más importancia histórica en este decenio es la constitución de la Confederación de Nacionalidades Indígenas del Ecuador (CONAIE) en 1986 como una conclusión y síntesis del proceso organizativo y de lucha indígena y, al mismo tiempo, como confirmación de la emergencia de un sector social invisible en la convivencia nacional e internacional desde muchos siglos atrás. Es decir, que con este acontecimiento se habría producido la realización de los sueños indios: la unidad de todos, por sobre las actitudes políticas y religiosas, sin descuidar la construcción de una unidad ideológica de los pueblos indígenas y sectores sociales y populares del país.

Durante esa misma etapa de los años 80 y como dentro de esta orientación, como una de las primeras demandas de la CONAIE, tuvo lugar la reforma del Estado a través de la convocatoria a una Asamblea Constituyente, llevada a cabo por medio de los mecanismos institucionales correspondientes. Estas exigencias estuvieron acompañadas con otras demandas concretas, como la legalización y resolución de los conflictos de tierra. Además, dentro del marco de la lucha de nuestros pueblos por el fortalecimiento de su identidad, está presente la propuesta de la educación intercultural bilingüe, la cual cobra importancia nacional por la intervención del Estado al institucionalizar este programa, aunque exclusivamente con dedicación a los pueblos indígenas.

En los inicios de la década de los 90, la actividad organizativa del movimiento indígena se centró en la elaboración de su propuesta política y la construcción de las estrategias y mecanismos de lucha, en perspectiva de su unidad interna y la ampliación del espacio de lucha en alianza con otros sectores, con miras a la redefinición de la estructura institucional y de la sociedad. En este contexto se explica el planteamiento y la realización histórica del Levantamiento de mayo y junio de 1990, el acontecimiento más grande en los últimos años del siglo y milenio anterior.

Las estrategias de la propuesta indígena

La sistematización de las experiencias y de todo un proceso dinámico de acciones es lo que permite visualizar y elaborar una *propuesta* global coherente política e históricamente en nombre de los pueblos indígenas y dirigida hacia el conjunto de la sociedad. El mérito de la iniciativa es que proviene de todo un acumulado histórico interno de lo indígena, así como de una reflexión política en dimensiones globales del mundo contemporáneo. Además, de la consideración de estos componentes fue esencialmente que se vislumbró la propuesta de la construcción de un Estado Plurinacional, y en función del cumplimiento a este mandato se diseñaron las siguientes estrategias y frentes de lucha.

En primer término, nuestro movimiento se avocó a la constitución de un frente social orgánica y funcionalmente sólido e ideológicamente invariable en su posición, planteándonos como una base fundamental la unidad estratégica de nuestros pueblos. Este sector social, tanto en su presencia cuantitativa y cualitativa, desde sus luchas y su confrontación a la institucionalidad, se ha convertido en un actor fundamental en la escena nacional e internacional. Al destacar los resultados de la acción del frente social representado por la CONAIE, podemos afirmar que con esta organización se logran avances importantes en la apertura y transformación de las estructuras institucionales. Es el caso de varios espacios indígenas con contenido innovadores, como la Dirección Nacional de Educación Intercultural Bilingüe (DINEIB) dentro del Ministerio de Educación y Cultura, reconocida en el año de 1988; el Consejo de Nacionalidades y Pueblos del Ecuador (CODENPE), establecido en la Presidencia de la República, y aceptado en 1997; la Dirección Nacional de Salud Indígena (DINASI), creada en el Ministerio de Salud Pública por un acuerdo Ministerial en 1999. Todos estos logros son resultado de las luchas de carácter institucional del movimiento indígena. En el marco de esta línea de acción también se ubica el haber podido arrancar la voluntad política de los diferentes gobiernos para la legalización de varios territorios indígenas en la Amazonía y la Costa, así como la resolución de los cientos de conflictos de tierras en el país, animados de una comprensión profunda del espacio territorial como es la visión indígena de la relación hombre-naturaleza y en este contexto la lucha se extiende a evitar la presencia de las compañías transnacionales cuyo fin es explotar los recursos naturales. Cabe mencionar que dichas conquistas y luchas siempre venían acompañadas de una serie de mecanismos de represión, como la persecución, la militarización generalizada, la prisión o muerte de hombres y mujeres líderes indígenas.

Otro frente importante en la lucha del movimiento indígena es el de la acción política. Desde hacía tiempo, se consideraba necesaria estratégicamente la participación indígena en el escenario político nacional, por lo que se evidenció entonces el surgimiento de un frente político representativo de nuestros pueblos. A finales de 1995, en una decisión colectiva se constituye el Movimiento de Unidad Plurinacional Pachakutik-Nuevo País como un medio y mecanismo de lucha y no como un fin estático. Fue así que esta propuesta del movimiento indígena para la sociedad se constituye en un instrumento válido para el establecimiento de alianzas con otros sectores y la ampliación del espacio de lucha indígena, así como la construcción de un poder alternativo a mediano y largo plazo en el Ecuador. En otras palabras, el movimiento se puede caracterizar como una necesidad de lucha, porque desde este frente de acción se pueden emprender gestiones políticas — cuyo espacio carece de vacíos – hasta entonces no emprendidas porque estos mecanismos no han sido bien utilizados históricamente en el pasado por los partidos políticos tradicionales. En materia de logros desde este frente, podemos decir que se vive un proceso cualitativo muy importante desde y hacia nuestros pueblos. La participación electoral de 1996 arrojó como resultados 75 autoridades a nivel nacional, entre ellos, 6 alcaldes, consejeros, concejales y 8 diputados. Pero más importante es resaltar la acción parlamentaria de nuestros representantes tanto por su consistencia ideológica como por el papel desempeñado durante su período; aún más, la gestión administrativa de los alcaldes ha sido reconocida y aplaudida por la opinión nacional e internacional.

Políticamente, la acción tanto desde el frente social como del frente político ha desempeñado un rol fundamental en los procesos de transformación y en los momentos de crisis nacional. Así, la denuncia y su gran poder de convocatoria han sido decisivos para definir algunos de los acontecimientos de más trascendencia en el Ecuador, por ejemplo, los derrocamientos de los dos gobiernos anteriores, el de Abdalá Bucaram y Jamil Mahuad. La acción política del movimiento indígena y popular procura una acelerada reforma y profundización de la democracia, y, a través de ella, el pueblo ecuatoriano ha experimentado una Asamblea Constituyente en 1988 en la que la Constitución Política del Estado sufrió cambios importantes, como la incorporación de los Derechos Colectivos, una iniciativa del movimiento indígena en función de ejercitar sus derechos propios y legítimos. Además, en la última participación político electoral en 1998, se advirtieron avances cualitativos significativos, y los resultados fueron satisfactorios. Esta vez fueron elegidos 27 alcaldes, 8 diputados, 5 prefectos, más de 50 concejales y consejeros, mientras que sobrepasó los 100 el número de miembros de las Juntas Parroquiales. Es decir, que el frente y la acción política junto a las luchas sociales están de avanzada en el Ecuador.

En otro orden y otros frentes, la estrategia del movimiento indígena señala con precisión el componente educativo, académico, y científico como una acción de fortalecimiento del desarrollo organizacional y para enfrentar el reto de la modernidad y el mundo globalizado. En base a la experiencia educativa de los pueblos indígenas, la propuesta de la educación superior es innovadora y de características particulares, tanto en su contenido, que incorpora en la estructura curricular los conocimientos a partir de las identidades locales junto a los conocimientos y ciencias universales, como en la metodología y las modalidades de enseñanza, que se dirigen a trasladar la universidad hacia la comunidad, es decir, a crear una universidad intercultural y descentralizada. Esta propuesta universitaria que ha sido un sueño de todos nuestros pueblos se encuentra en la fase de implementación, pero la tarea por delante es aplicar la estructura funcional de la universidad en el campo. Este nuevo modelo de universidad es otro de los aportes del movimiento indígena con dimensiones de cobertura regional en todo el área de la comunidad andina prioritariamente.

De manera que el crecimiento de un sector social como el de los indígenas se explica primeramente como el de una sociedad emergente que luego se ha convertido en actor social y progresivamente en actor político, con perspectivas a superar las adversidades del presente milenio.

Algunas de las luchas que dieron lugar a los levantamientos importantes del movimiento indígena fueron resultado de nuestras deliberaciones sobre decisiones gubernamentales, como las medidas económicas que obedecen a las políticas de ajustes impuestas por un modelo y que perjudican a un 80 por ciento de la población que se encuentra por debajo de la línea de la pobreza. Es el caso del levantamiento de enero del 2000. En cambio, en enero y febrero del 2001, la dolarización de la economía y el desmantelamiento del sistema financiero fueron los detonantes de la acción insurreccional. Además, este último acontecimiento generó como resultado el establecimiento del diálogo entre el gobierno y el movimiento indígena, pero de dichas conversaciones aún no se advierten resultados. Un logro que sí podemos atribuirnos es el respeto al mecanismo del diálogo como tal. La práctica del diálogo fue instaurada e impuesta en nuestro país desde la experiencia y exigencia indígena, por esto valoramos esta práctica como uno de los logros más positivos de nuestras acciones. Ningún otro sector le ha obligado en ningún momento a gobierno alguno a sentarse en la mesa del diálogo, y por lo tanto, éste ciertamente es un mérito más del movimiento indígena ecuatoriano desde 1990.

Finalmente, es importante señalar que la agenda del movimiento indígena en los momentos y realidades actuales se sintetiza como:

- Políticas de Estado, por ejemplo, el tratamiento de la Reforma del Estado;

- Temas nacionales, como el debate del Plan Colombia; y
- Temas indígenas, por ejemplo, el caso del Fondo Indígena, un asunto específico de los pueblos indígenas.

En fin, desde una perspectiva histórica, la posición que ha tomado el movimiento indígena ecuatoriano y las acciones pacíficas y transparentes de nuestro movimiento han incidido directa o indirectamente a nivel de los acontecimientos internacionales, desde su protagonismo en la lucha contestataria del quinto centenario de la colonización americana, atravesando los momentos del gran encuentro con otros pueblos y naciones del Abya Yala e incluyendo la constitución de la Coordinadora de Organizaciones y Naciones Indígenas del Continente (CONIC), y luego la presencia activa de los representantes indígenas del Ecuador en los foros de las Naciones Unidas y su participación en la elaboración de la declaración universal de los Derechos de los Pueblos Indígenas – todos éstos son aportes hacia el crecimiento cualitativo de un movimiento indígena a nivel internacional.

Para mí es un gran placer presentar el libro de Melina Selverston-Scher, *Ethnopolitics in Ecuador: Indigenous Rights and the Struggle for Democracy (La etnopolítica en Ecuador: Los derechos indígenas y la lucha por la democracia)*. La doctora Selverston-Scher ha acompañado a las organizaciones indígenas del Ecuador en su lucha durante la pasada década, y por lo tanto, ella conoce bien nuestra realidad. Hoy, pues, gracias a sus esfuerzos y a este libro, la historia de nuestro movimiento puede llegar al público de habla inglesa.

Foreword

LUIS MACAS

BACKGROUND

One of the deepest values held by indigenous peoples to this day undoubtedly is their capacity to resist the various adverse challenges thrust upon them by European colonization: their staunch resistance in the face of economic exploitation, political oppression, the state of exclusion, and social discrimination that are the legacy of colonialism. Our peoples maintain their values, knowledge, wisdom, and especially their own cultural, economic, and political institutions, against all adversities.

Such principles have given indigenous peoples and communities their inner life, and they have also determined the struggles, efforts, and achievements of the indigenous movement today. However, several indigenous institutions of a very diverse nature give our peoples their capacity for organization and social relations as well as their spirituality and intimate connection to mother nature. The *ayllu* (family), *ayllu llakta* (community), *minka* (collective work), *rimanakuy* (the practice of dialogue), *yuyarinakuy* (agreements), and *pacha mama* (nature) are vital sources of strength to these communities as they struggle for self-preservation and perfection in the modern world.

While the above institutions served as pillars in the construction of indigenous societies, they still stand as supports of the indigenous people's agendas to make deep changes in society and to build a state with a truly pluri-national identity. However, the indigenous peoples have also gleaned another complex dimension from their struggle, as a result of their coexist-

---

Dr. Luis Macas, Former President of the Confederation of Indigenous Nationalities of Ecuador (Confederación de las Nacionalidades Indígenas del Ecuador — CONAIE), is currently President of the University of Indigenous Nationalities and Peoples of Ecuador (Universidad Intercultural de las Nacionalidades y Pueblos Indígenas del Ecuador) and Director of the Institute for Science and Indigenous Cultures (Instituto Científico de Culturas Indígenas — ICCI).

This Foreword was translated by José Grave de Peralta, senior editor for English and Spanish publications, North-South Center Press at the University of Miami.

ence with the dominant class. They have assumed a position of self-awareness and class struggle. Based on this perspective and social consciousness, they have designed for themselves a set of tools to deal with society's more general and complex questions as a whole, for example, to define the concept of the state and the state's structures, the political system, and the restrictions placed on democracy today by inequality, injustice, and so on.

Two Lines of Action

The above topics were some of the organizing principles of the indigenous movement in the initial phase of its struggle. Based on this perspective and experience, our organizations have defined the following key strategies as their two fundamental lines of action:

- One of these lines of action is connected to the movement's historical-cultural — ethnic — dimension, expressed in demands for rights and immediate reforms that are fundamental for an endogenous agenda. In other words, in this sense, the struggles themselves are generated by the specific interests of the indigenous nations and peoples for legitimate and historical rights that have never been recognized by the state and the dominant society. These demands, however, are born in the very heart of these sectors. Some analysts view this dimension as a purely ethnic or anthropological issue that uses or prioritizes an ethnocentric or indigenous point of view to the exclusion of everything else.

- Another concept or line of action present in the Ecuadoran indigenous movement is related to its social dimension, the class struggle for identity within contemporary society. Indigenous peoples acquired their views and strategies based on their experiential understanding of social and political phenomena and the problems of the world surrounding them.

  The understanding of this dimension and its subsequent practice has been a constant behind the indigenous movement's strategies throughout its phase of organizational and ideological formation. Undoubtedly, this angle of social class consciousness is a fundamental part of the indigenous agenda, explaining why the indigenous movement has become a catalyst for and embodiment of the indigenous people's demands in general and, especially, why the movement is pivotal as a social actor for centralizing these demands and voicing the people's collective and global interests. Therefore, this social dimension articulates the Ecuadoran movement's ethnocultural and social class struggle.

Clearly, indigenous claims and efforts target both of the above dimensions or objectives. One area has to do with reforms, cultural issues, and immediate solutions, in other words, concrete interests proper to this sector, based on the specific needs of these nations, peoples, and communities. However, the scope of these reforms and these immediate and concrete demands is not exclusive or excluding, but rather it opens another line of action, with wider ramifications that are more global and aimed at contemporary social, economic, and cultural issues. The struggles of the indigenous movement are always aligned to the larger social context. That is, these struggles always have been closely identified with the demands of other social sectors and based on common objectives aimed at building a new state and society.

The Indigenous Struggle and Its Demands

An agenda of indigenous demands that is coherent and open to improvement must be based on the understanding and exercise of the two dimensions outlined above — a historical-cultural perspective and a place in the country's political and social activities — based on a questioning of state structures and of a social, economic, and political system that is inadequate, obsolete, and does not meet contemporary needs. In this sense, the indigenous movement's initiatives, in their demands and perspectives, are inclusive of all of society. Some of the agenda's most pressing demands are the following: reestablishing dialogue as a way to obtain consensus, the building of a pluri-national state, a reconciliation through intra-cultural awareness and social and cultural diversity, and the expansion and deepening of democracy, equality, and social justice.

It must be pointed out that the various struggles that took place throughout Ecuador's history during its colonial and republican periods were answers to what I would call the *postponement* of our peoples. I am referring to the great uprisings of Tupac Amarú,[1] Fernando Daquilema,[2] and others, leading up to the attempts at structural and historical reforms in the 1990s to give visibility to the indigenous movement in the Ecuadoran state and society and to obtain institutional recognition of the diversity, dignity, and rights of the indigenous peoples.

In describing the most important elements in the evolution and advancement of the indigenous movement, I would venture to say that *dignity* was the first *fundamental idea* of the movement during its initial and building phases — dignity was behind the struggle for land and territories and behind the quest to strengthen national identity, for example, through the recognition of the native languages and indigenous education.

These elements became determining factors of the movement during the 1950s and 1960s, a period of euphoria resulting from the institutionalization of communal lands for our peoples. On the one hand, legislation was unilaterally applied by the state to institutionalize the indigenous community or *ayllu llakta*. However, this legislation resulted in direct and vertical control by the state in our communties. From the movement's point of view this political measure was the imposition of an extraneous form of governance, explicitly intended to weaken our ancient communties. In Ecuador, this era also marked the beginning of communal or first-level organizations, as they are now called in the context of our indigenous society. The ayllu llakta, the community, is the most basic nucleus of indigenous society after that of family, and the term has an absolutely unique meaning for indigenous peoples.

During the 1950s and 1960s, the newly created agricultural communities, or comunas, especially affected the indigenous communities, but also the peasant and Afro-Ecuadoran populations of the country. However, the fact that the communal unit was institutionalized a number of years after the actual adoption of the Law of Agricultural Communities (Ley de Comunas) in 1936 is due to basic weaknesses inherent in the implementation of the law at the state level. These institutional problems called for a unique design according to the indigenous peoples' particular interests. This explains why the indigenous process went beyond the state's offers at that time and attempted to expand and reinforce the course of organizational development by structuring second- and third-level organizations as basic units of the indigenous process.

The reason for underscoring this particular early stage of organization and struggle in the indigenous process is the role it played in obtaining one of the key objectives of indigenous unity — recognition of ancestral and communal lands. In other words, the unity achieved in the struggle of indigenous peoples and their ability to obtain state recognition through the Ley de Comunas led to another victory, which was the Law of Agrarian Reform passed in 1964. In fact, this second confrontation with the state revealed the problem of *land ownership* as a constant theme and certainly one of the most contemporary and historical problems in the struggle.

The struggles of the 1970s resulted in the creation and establishment of third-level organizations and the creation of regional organizations. The main goal that the indigenous movement set for itself at that time was the recovery of indigenous lands in the Highlands region and the defense of indigenous territories in the Amazon and the Coast. The struggle for these territorial rights is being waged by provincial organizations as well as by ECUARUNARI (*Ecuador Runacunapac Riccharimui* – Ecuador Indians Awaken), a regional organization in the Andes that defines strategies for truly uniting all of Ecuador's peoples and, in turn, generating other target areas of reform, such as education, health, and other similar services.

The 1980s was undoubtedly one of the most important decades in the history of the indigenous peoples, a time full of significant qualitative changes. At that time, indigenous nations and peoples rediscovered themselves. They came together to hold a new, sustained dialogue, characterized by its openness and extensive subject matter, bringing together all of the sources they had for following up the indigenous movement's process. It was also a time for raising the indigenous peoples' awareness of themselves as a cultural entity and as a social class. Historically, the key event of that decade was the creation, in 1986, of the Confederation of Indigenous Nationalities of Ecuador (Confederación de las Nacionalidades Indígenas del Ecuador — CONAIE) as the culmination and synthesis of the indigenous struggle's organizational process. Additionally, CONAIE's creation marked the emergence of what had been an invisible social sector in the national and international scene for many centuries. In other words, CONAIE was the realization of the indigenous people's dream of uniting all indigenous people — overcoming all political and religious differences — and at the same time constructing an ideological unity encompassing all indigenous peoples and all social and popular sectors of Ecuador.

Within this context, one of the foremost demands of the CONAIE, during the 1980s, was the reformation of the Ecuadoran state, through the convocation of a Constituent Assembly that would carry out the reforms by institutionalized means. In addition, other concrete demands included the legalization and resolution of land disputes. In another important area, the CONAIE called for strengthening the national identity through bilingual intercultural education, which was raised to the level of national importance by the direct intervention of the state as it institutionalized the bilingual program, even though the program was aimed exclusively at the indigenous populations.

At the beginning of the 1990s, the indigenous movement's organization focused on elaborating its political agenda and building reform strategies and mechanisms in order to become more unified and widen the scope of its reforms by joining other sectors. This move to redefine Ecuador's institutional and social structure explains the historical event of the May and June 1990 Uprising, certainly the movement's biggest accomplishment at the close of the century and millennium.

The Strategies of the Indigenous Agenda

The indigenous movement's systematic review of its experiences and of the very complex, dynamic process involved allowed the movement to see and formulate a coherent global *agenda*, both politically and historically, in the name of indigenous peoples but directed at the larger context of society. The merit of this initiative is that it is the result both of an accumulation of historical, internal factors of what is truly indigenous and of political reflections about contemporary society on a global scale. The possibility of building a pluri-national country is based essentially on the consideration of these factors, and the movement has designated the following series of strategies and areas for carrying out the mandates of this agenda.

The first task is to create an internally and functionally solid social front, constant in its ideological position, based fundamentally on the strategic unity of our peoples. This social sector, both for quantitative and qualitative reasons, through its struggles and institutional confrontations, has become a fundamental actor both nationally and internationally. In terms of the social front's activities through the CONAIE, important strides have been made in opening and transforming existing institutional structures. Among these advancements are the creation of thoroughly innovative indigenous groups, like the National Directorate of Bilingual Intercultural Education (Dirección Nacional de Educación Intercultural Bilingüe — DINEIB), which became recognized in 1988 within the Ministry of Education and Culture; the Council for the Development of Nationalities and Peoples of Ecuador (Consejo de Desarrollo de las Nacionalidades y Pueblos del Ecuador — CODENPE), established by the president of the Republic and ratified in 1997; and the National Department of Indigenous Health (Dirección Nacional de Salud Indígena — DINASI) in the Public Health Ministry, ratified by a ministerial decree in 1999. All of the above may be considered institutional advancements made by the indigenous movement. Other significant results include obtaining the political approval from various governments to grant legal status to several indigenous territories in the Amazon and the Coast, as well as the resolution of hundreds of land disputes in Ecuador, inspired by a deep understanding of the territory, based on the indigenous vision of the relationship between man and nature, and resulting in the movement's opposition to the presence of transnational corporations that exploit those territories for their natural resources. It should be mentioned that all of the above victories and struggles were always accompanied by various mechanisms of repression, including persecution, generalized militarization, and the imprisonment or death of male and female indigenous leaders.

Another important front for the indigenous peoples is the political arena. In other words, our movement realized that it was strategically necessary to have indigenous participation at the national political level; this resulted in the creation of a political front for our peoples. At the end of 1995, by a unanimous decision, we created the Pachakutik-New Country Movement for Pluri-national Unity-New Country (Movimiento de Unidad Plurinacional Pachakutik-Nuevo País) as an instrument and means for change and not as an end in itself. This indigenous force aims to become a valid political instrument for establishing alliances with other sectors and expanding the indigenous process into other areas, as well as for building an alternative medium- and long-range force in Ecuador. The Pachakutik Movement may be called a necessary tool for change because the front allows us to take political actions that are not empty and to operate in a different way from the past, under the traditional party systems. In terms of achievements, we could say that the front has experienced a very important qualitative change for the benefit of our peoples. In 1996, the movement participated in elections, resulting in the victory of 75 indigenous authorities on a national level, including six mayors, eight representatives, and numerous counselors and councilmen. However, most important is the parliamentary work of our representatives, both for their ideological consistency and for the role they played during their terms in office. Also very important, the administrative work of the mayors has won national and international recognition.

Politically, the front, both in its social dimensions and in its political functions, has played a key role in the transformations and moments of national crisis that have taken place in Ecuador. Both the movement's voice and power to congregate large numbers have made decisive impacts on transcendental events, such as the overthrow of the governments of Abdalá Bucaram and Jamil Mahuad. The popular indigenous movement's political actions have been seeking to bring about accelerated reforms and a deepening of democracy. For example, in 1988, the Ecuadoran people experienced a Constituent Assembly that brought about important changes, such as the incorporation of collective rights into the Constitution of Ecuador, the result of the indigenous movement's desire to exercise their people's own legitimate rights. During the last elections in 1998, the movement's political advances were qualitatively significant and positive. For example, the elections yielded 27 mayors, 8 representatives, 5 provincial prefects, and more than 50 councilmen and counselors, and the number of indigenous members in town councils now exceeds 100. Clearly, the movement is at the forefront in the struggle both socially and politically.

In other areas, the indigenous movement has defined the importance of the front's educational and scientific component for strengthening the front's organization and indigenous people's ability to meet the challenges of today's global society. The indigenous movement's higher education reforms are innovative and unique, both in the way they combine the local native identities with universal knowledge and sciences in the curricula's design and in the way they use the best scientific and academic teaching methodologies and approaches. The idea is to take the university to the communities, thus making the university multicultural and decentralized. This type of university model, which has been the dream of all of our peoples, is still in its initial phase, but its basic goal is to extend the presence of the university into the rural regions of Ecuador. This goal is another of the indigenous movement's contributions on a regional level that will affect the entire Andean community.

The process described above illustrates the growth of the indigenous peoples as a social sector, first, as an emerging society and second, as a social and increasingly political actor on the way to overcoming the challenges of the new millennium.

Some of the issues that gave rise to Ecuador's major uprisings had to do with government decisions, such as economic measures dictated by policies based on a specific neoliberal model, which harmed the 80-percent component of the population who exist below the poverty line. This was the case in the January 2000 Uprising. By contrast, the January and February 2001 Uprising was triggered by the dollarization of the economy and the dismantling of the financial system. Even though there are as yet no results from these conversations, the 2001 Uprising resulted in a dialogue between the government and the indigenous movement. However, one valuable aspect of the dialogue that I would like to stress is the respect for this dialogue mechanism as such. Dialogue was established and made mandatory in our country as a valid *practice* based on the experiences and needs of the indigenous peoples, and it is considered one of the most positive outcomes of our movement. At no other time in Ecuador's history has the indigenous or any other sector obligated any government to sit down and hold a dialogue. This is a significant achievement of the Ecuadoran indigenous movement since 1990.

Finally, it is important to point out that the indigenous movement has the following three goals on its agenda at the present time:
- State policies, specifically, how to carry out state reforms;
- National policies, for example, the debate over Plan Colombia;
- Indigenous issues, the case of the Indigenous Fund, a specific topic of the indigenous peoples.

The historical stance taken by the Ecuadoran indigenous movement and its peaceful and transparent actions have made direct and indirect impacts on international events. For example, Ecuador's movement led the protests against the celebration of the 500-year anniversary celebration of the colonization of America and continued with the momentous meeting of Ecuador's indigenous people with other peoples and nations of Abya-Yala.[3] The movement's additional achievements include the formation of the Council of Indigenous Organizations and Nations of the Continent (Coordinadora de Organizaciones y Naciones Indígenas del Continente — CONIC) and the active presence of Ecuador's indigenous representatives in United Nations fora and their participation in the drafting of a universal declaration of the Rights of Indigenous Peoples. Through all of these actions, Ecuador's indigenous peoples have contributed significantly to the qualitative growth of the indigenous movement on an international level.

It is with great pleasure that I present *Ethnopolitics in Ecuador: Indigenous Rights and the Struggle for Democracy.* Dr. Melina Selverston-Scher has accompanied the indigenous organizations of Ecuador in their struggle over the past decade, and she knows our reality. Now, through her efforts, the story of our movement can be brought to the English-speaking public.

Notes

1. José Gabriel Condorcanqui (1740-1781), Tupak Amarú II, was a Peruvian indigenous revolutionary descended from the last Inca ruler, Tupak Amarú, with whom he was identified when he led his countrymen in an uprising against Spanish rule in the eighteenth century. His movement spread throughout southern Peru and into Bolivia, Ecuador, and Argentina.

2. Fernando Daquilema led a revolt in 1860 against dictator Gabriel García Moreno, who seized power in 1860 and served two terms as president (1861-1865 and 1869-1875) until he was assassinated by liberals in 1875.

3. See NativeWeb for a more detailed description of the term Abya Yala at <http://abyayala.nativeweb.org/about.php>. As explained in the web site, this indigenous name comes from the Kuna peoples of Panama and Colombia, and it "denominates the American continents in their entirety." The name has been proposed for use by "all indigenous peoples in the Americas ... in their documents and oral declarations" in order to avoid "subjecting [indigenous] identity to the will of [the non-indigenous] invaders."

Preface, Methodology, and Acknowledgments

PREFACE

Our bus was hurtling along the steep slopes of the Andean night. With characteristic intensity, Luis Macas, the inspirational leader of the Ecuadoran indigenous movement, explained to me the meaning of the name he had given his eldest son, Pachakutik. The literal translation from Quichua is "the return of time" or "rebirth."[1] The current usage comes from the Incan concept of the rebirth of the indigenous people. Contemporary indigenous organizations in Ecuador have led a rebirth by strengthening their political movement and their identity. They are creating what truly is a new indigenous presence in the country.

This book tells a story inspired by the indigenous people of Ecuador, not only because they are creating opportunities for themselves, but also because they offer alternative models for all of modern industrial society. In Latin America today, the indigenous movement provides hope to the powerless just as revolutionary movements did a few decades ago. Working with people who were active in the indigenous movement in Latin America was a satisfying and meaningful experience for me because I witnessed firsthand the positive changes that have resulted from their struggle. I hope that this study's political analysis will contribute to an understanding of the ethnocentrism that dominates political structures in most societies in Latin America and the Caribbean and will suggest approaches that may lead to positive changes.

METHODOLOGY

This book is based on field research completed during two periods: three months during the summer of 1991 and 13 months from September 1992 through October 1993. Additional research was carried out during brief visits in 1994 and 1995. During these periods in Ecuador, I conducted formal interviews with members of organizations and indigenous communities, teachers, and government representatives in the provinces of Imbabura, Loja, Bolívar, Pastaza, and Chimborazo. In each of the three case-study provinces, I interviewed, at a minimum, two communities (conducting group interviews with community leadership or with the associations representing parents of schoolchildren); the provincial federation leaders; and the director of bilingual education for the province, the governor, the prefect, and either the mayor or the political chief most important to the province. I also reviewed local newspapers in the three provinces from the periods of indigenous unrest (the 1990 and 1994 protests). Further formal interviews were conducted with national and regional indigenous organizations and national government representatives in Quito. The interviews focused on four themes: the organization process, the "1990 Indigenous Uprising" and its effects, indigenous political participation, and issues of identity. In addition, I conducted numerous informal interviews with indigenous and *mestizo* (mixed race) political actors and scholars. The reflections I gathered from those interviews form the basis of the following interpretations. (A complete list of formal interviews is included in Appendix 3 of this book.)

Ecuador was selected as a useful case study of indigenous politics because of the exceptional impact of Ecuador's indigenous movement on the country. Ecuador also is an ideal case because the variable of indigenous identity could be isolated from other factors, such as guerrilla or drug-trafficking activities, in explaining the country's social movement. Isolation of the identity variable would have been more difficult in Peru, Guatemala, or Colombia, for example. This study should have a bearing on the situation in other countries in the region with similar conditions, including a culturally diverse society, rural economy, and weak political institutions. The lessons about political systems in a multiethnic state gleaned from the Ecuadoran case should be useful for understanding other Latin American countries.

In the case of Ecuador, it is important to examine political relations at the provincial level in order to understand the effects of the indigenous movement. Ecuador remains a predominantly rural society. Half of the Ecuadoran people live in cities with populations larger than 500,000, and one-third live in the two largest cities, Quito and Guayaquil.[2] The legitimacy of the modern political systems that developed in these cities is less observable in the countryside, where traditional agrarian power structures prevail. For example, a recent electoral study concluded that abstentions or null votes have marked elections in regions with significant indigenous populations.[3] Thus, I considered it necessary to observe the political relationships of local government structures and indigenous movements in order to understand indigenous politics in contemporary Ecuador. Accordingly, I chose three provinces for comparative study of local politics: Loja, Bolívar, and Pastaza. These cases are interesting to compare because, despite their structural differences, they share the common variable of a strong indigenous movement.

By isolating the variable of indigenous identity, this study explains how identity politics has led to an increase in citizenship rights as well as material gains for indigenous communities in Ecuador. This research demonstrates that the indigenous movement in Ecuador has successfully challenged the exclusionary political system and has taken steps toward creating a government loyal to all its citizens. Political science debates about Latin America and the Caribbean have largely ignored the issue of ethnic diversity. My contention is that ethnic political movements, as demonstrated by the indigenous organizations in Ecuador, may make significant contributions to the development of participatory citizenship, which is essential to democracy. I hope this research will encourage further analysis of political models that will accommodate ethnic diversity and, in turn, lead to democratic stability.

The author interviews indigenous cooperative members.

ACKNOWLEDGMENTS

I am grateful to the Confederation of Indigenous Nationalities of Ecuador (Confederación de las Nacionalidades Indígenas del Ecuador—CONAIE) and its affiliates throughout the country for their generous contributions to this study. I also wish to thank Professor Douglas Chalmers and Professor Anthony Marx of Columbia University for their support and their engaging comments about my work. The Latin American Faculty of Social Sciences-

Ecuador Office (Facultad Latino Americana de Ciencias Sociales — FLACSO-Ecuador) provided an institutional base in Ecuador. The Institute for Latin American and Iberian Studies at Columbia University, the Tinker Foundation, and the Organization of American States (OAS) provided financial support. In Colombia, I benefited from the assistance of the Andean Commission of Jurists (Comisión Andina de Juristas), the National Indigenous Organization of Colombia (Organización Nacional Indígena de Colombia — ONIC), and the Regional Indigenous Council of Cauca (Consejo Regional Indígena del Cauca — CRIC). Chris Peters at the Seventh Generation Fund and Susan Benson at the Trust for the Americas also provided special support at key moments. Many friends and colleagues assisted with insightful discussions. In particular, I thank Jennifer Collins, Margaret Ovenden, Jo-Marie Burt, Rayda Márquez, Monique Segarra, Jorge León, León Zamosc, Cathy Schnieder, Jonathan Fox, Tanya Korovkin, Luis Macas, Humberto Muenala, Fabián Muenala, Leonardo Viteri, Laura Amagandi, Valvina Macas, Charles David Kleymeyer, and the staff of CONAIE. All of these sources enriched my analysis; however, I am fully responsible for the text presented here.

I consider myself lucky to have received the assistance and supportive comments from the North-South Center Press, especially Karen Payne, Kathleen Hamman, José Grave-de-Peralta, and Mary Mapes.

Thanks also to my colleagues at the Coalition for Amazonian Peoples and their Environment (Coalición para los Pueblos Amazónicos y su Medio Ambiente), especially David Rothschild, for their support through the last stages of writing. To my family, thank you for always believing in me. To Eddie Scher, not only did you help edit, you also gave me a good reason to finish the project.

Notes

1. Quichua is the Ecuadoran form of Quechua, the language of the Inca empire.

2. David Corkill and David Cubitt, 1988, *Ecuador: Fragile Democracy* (London: Latin America Bureau).

3. CEPLAES (Centro de Planificación y Estudios Sociales), 1996, *Proyecto de Investigación Pueblos Indígenas y Participación Electoral: Informe Final* (Quito).

Chapter 1

Introduction

At the turn of the new century, the indigenous movement arguably is the most important social movement in Ecuador. Workers, women, students, peasants, environmentalists, artists, and other groups have formed social movements that influence civil society in Ecuador, but none of these forces has demonstrated the momentum of the indigenous movement. Simultaneously, the indigenous movement seized control of education in the countryside; successfully challenged economic privatization of the agricultural sector; paralyzed commerce in the country through mass protests; and led civil society movements that ousted two presidents, Abdala Bucarám (1996-1997) and Jamil Mahuad (1998-2000).[1] Before 1990, most observers would have described the indigenous communities of Ecuador's Highlands as docile and passive — an image incompatible with their current position as a political force in society. By most accounts, before the movement was organized, the indigenous people were well on their way toward integration into the dominant Ecuadoran culture. During the 1990s, however, the indigenous movement became a central force influencing the terms of the political debate in Ecuador. How can this be explained?

Most recently, in January 2000, the indigenous movement gave a convincing display of its leadership in Ecuador's civil society. Severe economic crisis had led to a national political crisis. The world watched as the country braced itself for the riots and violence that often accompany political upheaval in Latin America. Instead, the indigenous movement led a sector of the military and other social actors in a peaceful solution: Together, these groups stepped into the vacuum of power and took over the government. Five thousand indigenous activists converged in Quito, the capital, to call for the resignation of the president, the Congress, and the Supreme Court, because the three branches of government were unable to handle the economic disaster that was bankrupting the country. Without violence or bloodshed, the protestors spontaneously occupied the government buildings, declaring themselves the new governing body: the Junta of National Salvation (Junta de Salvación Nacional). After fewer than 24 hours of coalition rule by the indigenous movement and the military, President Jamil Mahuad was forced to resign, the military command withdrew from the Junta, and power was turned over to Vice President Gustavo Noboa. The potentially violent situation was defused peacefully. For the first time in

1

modern Latin America, a military-indigenous alliance seized political power. Though momentous, the events were not surprising, considering the tremendous growth in influence of the indigenous political voice during the 1980s and 1990s.

The growth of the modern indigenous movement across Latin America is particularly noteworthy in Ecuador, which has become a continental center for indigenous organizing in recent years. However, the phenomenon can be observed throughout the hemisphere. In the context of weak political institutions, drastic economic measures, irrational exploitation of natural resources (frequently located in indigenous territories), and an international human rights movement that lends increasing support to ethnic minorities, the indigenous movements of Latin America are intensifying their political demands. As political analyst Deborah Yashar has noted, "Latin America's indigenous movements provide a mirror to the weak process of democratization and state building in the countryside and the deleterious effects that the current transition has had on indigenous communities."[2]

A growing literature documents the way civil society is organizing in Latin America, particularly given the context of new democracies that allow for the sustained growth of social movements, efforts at trade liberalization, emerging international networks, and the weakening of the traditional left. The indigenous movement in Ecuador exemplifies these movements as a modern social response to the macro transformations in society, economics, and politics. Even so, the indigenous political challenge is as old as European contact with the Americas, giving it a unique character and legitimacy.

Considering the importance of indigenous movements in Latin America, very little political analysis has been undertaken to examine them. Scholars interested in learning about these movements depend largely on anthropological analysis, some of which provides useful political frameworks.[3] In general, however, anthropological methods are inadequate for answering many of the political science questions raised by these movements. Political analysis has evolved since the continental commemorations of the 1992 quincentennial anniversary of the arrival of Christopher Columbus.[4] However, these contributions assign primary importance to the contextual factors that give rise to indigenous movements rather than describe the political significance of the movements.

This book analyzes the contemporary indigenous movement in Ecuador and its impact on emerging democratic systems. Political analysis regarding ethnic conflict in general has promoted the perspective that ethnic-based movements are detrimental to the political and economic development of a society. Based on my research, I propose a different view: In Ecuador, ethnic mobilization has strengthened democratic political systems. Ecuador provides evidence that ethnic-based movements can have a positive role in building and expanding democracy around the world.

Ethnic minorities throughout the world often are disenfranchised by their governments. Indigenous people in Latin America, through their modern organizations, are demanding opportunities to exercise their right to participate as citizens in society. In the Ecuadoran case, indigenous organizations are striving for a participatory model with the potential to lead to a more stable democratic system that accommodates the multiethnic nature of the country.

The extent of indigenous unrest in the Americas gained the attention of the world press most dramatically with the Zapatista Uprising in Mexico in January 1994, on the day the North American Free Trade Agreement (NAFTA) went into effect. Analysts were quick to note that this was neither a traditional Central American guerrilla insurgency in the Marxist-Leninist tradition nor a peasant revolt demanding land for those who work it. The Zapatista army demanded political reforms to support the rights of the country's 8 million indigenous people.[5] Similarly, albeit less violently, indigenous organizations throughout the Americas are achieving political reforms in their favor. These include legalization of and public funding for bilingual education in native languages, land rights, constitutional reforms and indigenous participation in constitutional assemblies, and experiments in autonomous indigenous political and judiciary systems. Most recently, indigenous movements are demanding protection from the impacts of economic liberalization. Still, the vast majority of the region's indigenous peoples are disenfranchised politically and economically. One of the most lucid examples of this exclusion is indigenous peoples' lack of legal title to their land throughout the Americas.

Indigenous people in Ecuador consider themselves excluded in many ways from the benefits of participation in the Ecuadoran political system. From their perspective, the Ecuadoran nation-state is modeled after a European model and represents the *mestizo*, or mixed, culture.[6] To be a participant, or a citizen, it was understood for decades that one had to sacrifice indigenous identity and acculturate, that is, adopt the dominant mestizo culture.[7] In effect, I contend, indigenous people were excluded from the rights of citizenship because they maintained their identity.

The modern indigenous movement developed and spread a new political ideology that insists on citizenship rights for indigenous people without sacrificing any elements of their ethnic identity.[8] In fact, the legitimacy of their demands for political participation is based on their identity as the original inhabitants of the country and their role as the sector of the population that puts food on urban tables. This ethnonationalist ideology calls for the government to recognize that Ecuador is a multiethnic, or, in the indigenous movement's language, a "pluri-national" country. In a pluri-national country, I suggest, the government should be equally loyal to all of its citizens, regardless of ethnicity. Just as the government expects all citizens to be loyal to the country, the government must also demonstrate its loyalty to all citizens "Ethnic homogeneity" is a condition for national stability that Dankwart Rustow highlighted in his seminal article on democratic transitions.[9] Within the political concept of a pluri-national state, democracy does not require ethnic homogeneity, but rather, an understanding on the part of the citizens that the state is loyal to all ethnic groups. By demanding equal political participation and holding the government accountable to them as citizens, indigenous people in Ecuador are building what some scholars of citizenship call the "civic community."

BACKGROUND

E cuador is a small Andean country that has been called an "island of peace" between its violence-ridden neighbors, Peru and Colombia.

Amazonian peoples are defending their territory.

Ecuador has experienced many of the political trends that have been observed elsewhere in Latin America but generally without the extreme results. For instance, although Ecuador had military governments, it was without the military despotism of the Southern Cone. Though considered a "banana republic" for many years, Ecuador did not experience direct U.S. interventions to protect U.S. interests, nor did it develop the extreme economic dependence on the United States that was observed in Central America and the Caribbean. Although Ecuador continues to benefit from oil reserves that have promised wealth since the early 1970s, the majority of the population continues to live below the poverty level established by the United Nations Educational, Scientific, and Cultural Organization (UNESCO). Guerrilla movements have appeared, but they have not led to civil wars. Populism continues to be an important political force but has not caused the mass unrest experienced in neighboring countries. Ecuador's relative stability generally has kept it out of the headlines and absent from systematic studies of the region. Yet, as David Corkill and David Cubitt have noted: "The same reasons that make Ecuador not a 'notorious' country also make it especially worth examining as a Latin American one. In some ways it is the most purely 'typical' Latin American republic."[10]

Ecuador is a rural country with a population of approximately 10 million people, divided into three regions, the Coast, the Highlands, and the Amazon. The Coast is the center of export agriculture, including bananas, sugar, coffee, and African palm. Over half of Ecuador's total population live in the Coastal region. The sprawling port city of Guayaquil has a population of over 2 million people, significantly larger than that of the Highlands' capital, Quito, with 1.5 million. The Highlands region, also known as the Sierra, is predominantly agricultural, with production primarily for domestic consumption, consisting mostly of precolonial livestock and products, such as llamas, potatoes, and maize. The Amazon region, which encompasses nearly half of Ecuador's land area, contains an important source of the country's wealth: petroleum. The tropical rain forest was inhabited almost solely by indigenous communities until oil drilling began in 1967, bringing roads, rapid colonization by mestizos, and accompanying disease. The settlers brought fruit, dairy, and African palm production to the region, but oil remains the driving force of the economy. However, the wealth generated by oil extraction is rarely reinvested into development of the Amazon region.

The majority of the indigenous population of Ecuador resides in the rural Highlands, working as subsistence farmers or artisans. In the Amazon region, indigenous people constitute the majority of the population outside the small urban outposts, and they live in dispersed communities or have isolated nomadic lifestyles. Small indigenous communities inhabit the Coastal region as well. There is no accurate count of the total indigenous population of Ecuador. Throughout the Americas, indigenous identity is transitional, making census difficult. The history of colonization, the continued economic and religious pressure to acculturate, and the social dominance of mestizo culture continue to confuse attempts to define the specific percentage of the population that is indigenous. A recent analysis notes that there is "an absence of statistical data collected with the express goal of measuring the ethnic variable."[11] The most commonly used statistic estimates that 40 percent of the Ecuadoran population are indigenous people.[12] The largest indigenous group is the Quichua, which predominates in the Highlands. The Amazon region includes Lowland Quichua as well as Shuar, Achuar, Secoya, Siona, Huaorani, and Cofán nationalities. Tsachila,

Chachi, and Awa communities are found on the Coast. Also, most members of a significant Afro-Ecuadoran ethnic group, about 5 percent of the total population, live in the Coastal region.

Throughout this book, the most prominent indigenous organization at the national level, the Confederation of Indigenous Nationalities of Ecuador (Confederación de las Nacionalidades Indígenas del Ecuador — CONAIE) will be discussed. According to Ecuador's Ministry of Education and Culture, CONAIE represented 70 percent of the indigenous population in 1992. CONAIE was formed in 1986 to unite indigenous federations from each province. The engine behind the 1990 National Indigenous Uprising, described in chapter 4, CONAIE rapidly became the national and international representative of Ecuador's indigenous people and the political center of the indigenous movement.

ORGANIZATION OF PRODUCTION

This is a study of the indigenous population in a predominantly rural society. Therefore, it is important to begin with a general understanding of the social relations of production, which provide the context for the indigenous movement. The majority of indigenous people are engaged in small-scale farming,and their primary political slogan is a cry for "land for those who work it." According to a 1991 study of rural organization in Ecuador, 75 percent of the country's arable land is dedicated to cattle pasture, with relatively low output. In addition, while the *campesinos* (farmers), almost all of whom are indigenous, supply most of the agricultural produce for Ecuadorans' domestic consumption, they control only 30 percent of the arable land.[13] Approximately 80 percent of the indigenous population live in poverty. Presumably, most of the remaining 20 percent are engaged in other forms of business, for example, in the production and marketing of cultural products such as textiles or music or in the informal urban labor sector.

Indigenous people in Ecuador speak of the *pacha mama* (mother earth) in the same way as countless other indigenous cultures around the world do. Their science, language, religion, history, and customs are all linked to a specific territory with which they identify deeply. The reasons indigenous communities remain on their land despite extremely exploitative conditions may have as much to do with these cultural ties as with economic factors.

Until recently, agricultural production in the Highlands was based on the feudal *huasipungo* (debt-peonage farm) system. Large farm (*hacienda*) owners provided subsistence plots and grazing land to families in exchange for their labor. Sometimes a small wage was included. When no wage was included, the system was designated as *arrimado* (bondage). Since the indigenous farmers were always indebted to the hacienda owners, they were tied to the land. While the workforce in the Coastal region of Ecuador shifted to wage labor with export agriculture, the Highlands remained in semifeudal production patterns. As late as 1954, "landless wage laborers represented only 2 percent of the agrarian workforce in this region."[14] A legacy of these haciendas in Latin America is the existence of poor indigenous communities around large farms, where the people continue to be employed as wage-laborers. Population pressures create economic stress for these rural families. Concurrently, the large landowners increasingly are absentee landowners. While some unused agricultural land was distributed through state-led agrarian reform processes in 1964 and 1973, according to Paola Sylva Charvet, that land amounts to only 8 percent of the arable land. The land grants given out averaged only 3.5 hectares in the Highlands, and often the land was of low quality and insufficient for a family's subsistence.[15] The significant amount of remaining unused, arable land is the target of many indigenous protests and land takeovers, as described below.

Indigenous people have engaged in land takeovers throughout Ecuador's history. The marked difference today is that a national movement under the leadership of CONAIE coordinates land takeovers. This network of organized indigenous federations not only provides the opportunities for collective action; it also provides a common ideology with which to understand such actions. A land takeover, for example, is understood under the new ideology as a "land recuperation." In today's Ecuador, indigenous people are reclaiming what they believe should have been theirs from the start: the right to own land, receive fair wages, and participate as equal citizens in a nation that respects all ethnic groups.

POLITICAL SYSTEM

Ecuador has seen transfers of power between civil and military regimes throughout much of its existence as a republic. An oil boom in the 1970s helped stabilize the economy. Peaceful transfers of power have taken place through elections since 1979, the year in which José María Velasco Ibarra,[16] one of Ecuador's most influential political leaders, died. A leader for nearly four decades, Velasco can be credited with the legacy of populist politics that still reigns in the country today. Leaders are elected based on charisma and their promises to alleviate the conditions of the large poor sector rather than on specific economic or administrative platforms. Ecuadoran politics have been described as "a system of relationships that rests on, and integrates, social status, economic predominance, regional loyalties, and ethnic character."[17]

Ecuador now functions under a presidential system organized under the 1978 Constitution, which includes several measures to promote political and social stability. The president serves for a single four-year term and must belong to a political party. The president is elected by a run-off vote between the two leading candidates to ensure majority support for the presidency, since there are about 20 political parties, varying with each election. The single-chamber Congress houses 57 provincial representatives and 12 nationally elected deputies. The president has veto and plebiscite power as well as the right to appoint a cabinet.

Ecuador has 22 provinces, each with a governor appointed by the president. In the name of the president, the governor names a political chief and a chief of police for each canton in the province. A canton is a political administrative unit based around an urban center. Each canton is divided into parishes, and each parish has its own political lieutenant, also named by the governor. Parallel to the executive administration, each province holds direct elections for an independent Chamber of Deputies and a Municipal Council.

In rural areas, indigenous communities have their own legal political identity, called a *comuna* (officially recognized agricultural community). The *comuna* system was established in 1937 by the Ley de Comunas (law recognizing agricultural communities). The *comuna* provides an administrative unit for the government to deal with rural communities. The appointed leadership of a *comuna* is called a *cabildo*. These administrative units were necessary to present land claims to the Ecuadoran Institute for Agrarian Reform and Colonization (Instituto Ecuatoriano de Reforma Agraria y Colonización — IERAC). The number of *comunas* rapidly increased during the Jaime Roldós administration.[18] *Comunas* are still the fundamental political unit for most indigenous communities, although many have united to form production associations and most joined indigenous federations during the 1980s.

The preceding general political and socioeconomic background provides the context for this book's discussion of the indigenous political movement in Ecuador. An organized social movement can influence a predominantly rural country that has relatively weak political institutions, as the research undertaken for this study demonstrates. The following overview of chapters summarizes the scope of the research and analysis.

OVERVIEW

Chapter 2 presents the idea of the indigenous movement as an ethnonationalist movement and reviews relevant analytical debates about nation-state development, democracy, and ethnicity. An inherent contradiction exists between the government-led nation-building model and the ethnic diversity present in most societies; this disparity can lead to political conflict. However, I suggest that the model and the diversity are not mutually exclusive, nor will they necessarily lead to violence. In fact, the model and the diversity may be complementary to the extent that their common objective is a pluralist form of democracy. In literature regarding the development of democratic institutions, ethnic mobilization often is considered a deterrent to democracy. I contend that ethnic mobilization can, in fact, lead to more democratic systems. In order to build democracy, it is essential for the various ethnic groups in a country to believe that the government is equally loyal to each of them.

Chapter 3 discusses the recent history of relations between the Ecuadoran government and indigenous communities, focusing primarily on the period during which the indigenous movement was consolidated as a political force in the country, from the Roldós administration through the Sixto Durán administration.[19] This chapter describes the formation of contemporary indigenous organizations in response to increasing state intervention in their communities. Evidence is also offered demonstrating that the indigenous movement has won important political space for its constituents within Ecuador, which, in turn, has spurred the growth of the movement, as indigenous people discovered the utility of their identity-based voice.

Chapter 4 analyzes the historic 1990 Indigenous Uprising that put indigenous people on the political map in Ecuador. Social movement literature is used to examine the political opportunity structures of the indigenous organizations. The analysis concludes that the movement has generated political openings making it in the best interests of indigenous communities to identify with the national indigenous political organization.

Chapter 5 details the development of an indigenous ideology that was propagated through bilingual literacy campaigns in the 1980s. I argue that identity politics leads to indigenous people's increased participation in civil society, illustrated by two events: the indigenous rollback of a state-sponsored agricultural policy that would have threatened small farmer subsistence and the weakening of political controls in the countryside by the appointment of independent indigenous teachers.

Chapter 6 analyzes indigenous-state relations in three Ecuadoran provinces: Loja, Pastaza, and Bolívar. The comparison suggests that local authorities are responding to indigenous questions in different ways; yet by responding to indigenous demands for representation, each province is creating political opportunities for civil society participation. Despite structural differences in the three regions, there is a unified movement based on indigenous identity. The indigenous goal of citizenship via participation in the realm of local politics is examined, followed by analysis that demonstrates that the indigenous movement is taking steps toward citizenship.

Chapter 7 summarizes the conclusions of this research and presents general arguments. The indigenous movement in Ecuador during the 1980s and 1990s opened a political space for indigenous Ecuadorans to participate in local and national politics. Indigenous leaders developed an identity-based ideology that mobilized the indigenous population, which previously had been excluded from political participation. Inherently, as excluded actors, their main demand is for inclusion or political participation, which can benefit democratic development. In their struggles for basic rights as citizens, the indigenous people of Ecuador have undermined patron-client structures, potentially clearing the way for increasingly democratic systems in the society as a whole. The indigenous people's demand for political participation as equal members of civil society — without sacrificing their cultures — challenges the assumption that cultural hegemony is required for democracy. It is my contention that the government must be equally loyal to the diverse cultures it governs in order to establish a pluralist democracy. The literature on social movements generally has focused on the emergence of those movements and what they mean to the participants. The research and analysis in this book demonstrate that collective action can have a significant impact on a political system. In the case of Ecuador, the contemporary indigenous movement has contributed to the building of a stronger, more inclusive civil society.

Notes

1. While the media portrayed the event as a military coup, it was, in fact, characterized by massive civil society demonstrations led by the indigenous movement. The military joined in order to have some control over the transition. See Melina Selverston-Scher, 2000, "Ecuador Paralyzed: Indigenous Call to End Corruption," *Native Americas* (Spring).

2. Deborah Yashar, 1997, *Indigenous Politics and Democracy: Contesting Citizenship in Latin America*, Working Paper #238 (July) (Notre Dame, Ind.: University of Notre Dame, The Helen Kellogg Institute for International Studies).

3. For example: Kay Warren, 1993, *The Violence Within: Cultural and Political Opposition in Divided Nations* (Boulder, Colo.: Westview Press); Greg Urban and Joel Sherzer, 1991, *Nation-States and Indians in Latin America* (Austin, Texas: University of Texas Press); and Charles Hale, 1994, *Resistance and Contradiction: Miskitu Indians and the Nicaraguan State, 1894-1987* (Stanford, Calif.: Stanford University Press).

4. Alison Brysk and Deborah Yashar have made notable contributions. See Alison Brysk, 1994, "Acting Globally: Indian Rights and International Politics in Latin America," in *Indigenous Peoples and Democracy in Latin America*, ed. Donna Lee Van Cott (New York: St. Martin's Press); Alison Brysk, 2000, *From Tribal Village to Global Village: Indian Rights and International Relations in Latin America* (Stanford, Calif.: Stanford University Press); Yashar 1997; and Deborah Yashar, 1999, "Democracy, Indigenous Movements, and the Post-Liberal Challenge in Latin America," *World Politics* 52 (1).

5. See Neil Harvey, 1999, *The Chiapas Rebellion: The Struggle for Land and Democracy* (Durham, N.C.: Duke University Press), for a detailed description of the Zapatista movement.

6. *Mestizo* is the term used throughout Latin America to describe the ethnic group of mixed Hispanic and indigenous people. I use the term "indigenous people" when referring to the descendants of the original inhabitants of the continent. "Indian" is considered derogatory in general, but some indigenous groups have reclaimed it as a term to describe the common struggle of many diverse peoples.

7. Linda Belote and Jim Belote describe this process and the recent transformations in their 1984 article, "Drain from the Bottom: Individual Ethnic Identity Change in Southern Ecuador," *Social Forces* 63 (1).

8. By citizenship rights, I refer to free and fair access to participate in political decision-making processes and to receive benefits from the government system.

9. Dankwart Rustow, 1970, "Transitions to Democracy," *Comparative Politics* (April): 337-363.

10. Corkill and Cubitt 1988, 1.

11. León Zamosc, 1993, "Protesta agraria y movimiento indígena en la Sierra Ecuatoriana," in *Sismo étnico en el Ecuador: Varias perspectivas*, ed. CEDIME (Centro de Investigaciones de los Movimientos Sociales del Ecuador) (Quito: Abya-Yala), 5.

12. Corkill and Cubitt 1988.

13. Paola Sylva Charvet, 1991, *La organización rural en el Ecuador* (Quito: Abya-Yala), 239.

14. José Vicente Zevallos, 1990, "Reforma agraria y cambio estructural: Ecuador desde 1964," *Ecuador Debate* 20: 42.

15. Sylva Charvet 1991.

16. José María Velasco Ibarra was elected as president five times but completed only one of those terms (1952-1956).

17. Corkill and Cubitt 1988, 3.

18. Jaime Roldós Aguilera (1979-1981).

19. Sixto Durán Ballén (1992-1996).

Chapter 2

Nationalism and Indigenous Politics in Latin America

INTRODUCTION

History has demonstrated that nationalism can be an important tool for political mobilization on the part of the state. Nationalist and, in this case, ethnonationalist ideology can be an important political resource for civil society as well. The case of Ecuador suggests that ethnonationalist movements may arise in postcolonial contexts, due in part to the inherent contradictions of nation building in a multiethnic society. This case also suggests that ethnonationalist movements can promote the resolution of potential political conflicts through further definition of the role of the state.

This chapter examines the question of nation-state development as it relates to Latin America, indigenous people, and the case of Ecuador in particular. In an ethnically diverse society in which one ethnic group is dominant in politics or in which an ethnic group is excluded from equal participation in civil society, conflict is likely to ensue. For such a society to establish a peaceful democracy, the state as an institution must accept cultural pluralism. This proposition challenges the supposition, held by many government officials and scholars, that cultural hegemony is a necessary requisite for contemporary democracy.

This chapter brings together the literature on nationalism, which tends to exclude Latin America, and the literature on building democracy in the region, which tends to exclude discussion of ethnic political mobilization. Noting the conjunction of the two schools of thought, the points made herein attempt to contribute to the richness of both. In addition, the exercise will provide a framework useful for an analysis of indigenous movements overall in Latin America and particularly in Ecuador.

NATION-STATES AND NATIONALIST MOVEMENTS

Definitions

A wide range of interpretations addresses the concepts and the sorts of questions relevant to the study of nationalism: What is a nation? What is nationalism? Is nationalism natural or forced? Good or evil? For some individuals, the mention of nationalism evokes images of Adolf Hitler's Germany, where anyone who did not fit into a socially accepted norm or particular ethnic or religious category was in danger of being sent to a death camp. For others, nationalism is a political project or a fundamental link to modernity. Let us briefly examine the meaning of these concepts as used in this book.

The "nation" continues to be an ambiguous concept in most social theory. The term is defined most commonly by its subjective characteristics, such as a people's awareness of their national identity. We can use the definition of nation offered by Anthony Smith: "a named human population sharing an historic territory, common myths and historical memories, a mass public culture, a common economy, and common legal rights and duties for all members."[1] This definition allows for an indigenous group to consider itself a nation. Particularly in North America, where indigenous peoples are sovereign, they self-identify as nations. In Latin America, it also is common to use the term "nationality" — a derivative of "nation" that connotes a national identity without a corresponding state apparatus. Since the Geneva Convention defined the basic human rights of peoples, ethnic groups have sought to be recognized as "peoples" to ensure their rights under the international political regime.[2]

Nation building is the process of forging a unified nation, usually from different cultures, to create the citizenship of a state and promote the efficiency considered necessary for success in the modern industrial world. State leaders, bolstered by intellectual, political, and economic interests, carry out the nation-building process. For some authors, such as Benedict Anderson, the process of nation building is largely passive, a result of the spread of vernacular language and markets.[3] For our purposes in this study, nation building is defined both as a process of the spread of homogenizing language and culture and the active project of the elite to build a unified nation-state.

"Ethnonationalism" is a subset of nationalism. The ideological movement called "nationalism" can be about protecting an existing nation or building a new one.[4] That nation can be defined around a modern identity (as in multiethnic Switzerland) or an ethnic identity (such as African-American). Ethnic nationalism can be secessionist, but its objective is not necessarily to obtain a separate state. As a social movement ideology, ethnonationalism can focus on obtaining special rights and recognition to protect an ethnically defined group. The contemporary indigenous movement is an ethnonationalist movement, in that it is organized around the principle of strengthening indigenous identity. However, most literature about nationalism considers nationalist mobilization to be a form of politics directed at controlling the modern state. To avoid confusion, this book's analysis generally refers to the indigenous movement as an ethnic political mobilization.[5]

THE NATION-STATE IN CONTEMPORARY POLITICS

The homogeneous nation-state apparently has not been consolidated. In most of the world today, ethnic allegiances still motivate power struggles and regulate inequalities in society. In fact, ethnic conflict may account for most of the organized violence in the modern world. While international politics continues to be coordinated largely through the nation-state system, the authority of nation-states is challenged by supranational trade alliances and multinational corporations and also by national liberation and secessionist movements.[6] Countries continue to be torn apart by ethnic conflicts.

Is the nation-state obsolete, either as a theoretical construct or as an actual political actor? I do not believe so. However, the nation-state concept should be modified to reflect the multiethnic reality of most countries and the changing role of national governments in international politics. As Anthony Smith has aptly noted, "In a world of competing states and would-be nations, these are no mere academic issues."[7] Scholarship has emphasized the apparent contradiction between ethnic identity and nation-state consolidation that often leads to conflict. The following analysis of the indigenous movement in Ecuador suggests that while the movement emerges out of this contradiction, ethnic allegiance and national citizenship need not be mutually exclusive.

To understand the growth of the indigenous movement over the last decade, it is helpful to consider it in the context of nation-building projects in the region. Although little reference to Latin America is made in the political science literature on nationalism, it is possible to apply theoretical models to the region.[8]

Why is Latin America on the fringe of this literature on nationalism? First, scholars of the region generally analyze Latin American social movements within class-based paradigms, focusing on the politics of institution-building and electoral processes, and, of course, on the regionally important processes of democratic transition from military rule. Moreover, while ethnic conflict has always been present during the national era, in Latin America it has rarely been the basis of violent challenges to state control as in other continents.[9] In addition, the founding of the Latin American republics has been considered successful, and scholars have assumed the cohesion of the Latin American nations.

In contrast, I contend that many Latin American countries can be considered incomplete nations, with weak consolidation of national identity, in which much of the population does not participate in the political system or benefit from citizenship. In many cases, a single ethnic group controls the government. In the case of Ecuador, a history of economic and social segregation of indigenous people laid the groundwork for continued political exclusion that led to the current ethnic conflicts. Therefore, to understand the contemporary political implications of the indigenous movement in Ecuador, it is important to consider the context of ethnic conflict and the nation-state.

NATIONALISM AND ETHNONATIONALISM IN LATIN AMERICA

Early indigenous resistance opposed colonization in general; only in recent decades have indigenous protests begun to focus on the demand for recognition of rights as citizens. Independence wars generally were waged in cities, and indigenous communities survived on the periphery; nevertheless, there was some important indigenous participation. The Peruvian indigenous philosopher José Carlos Mariátegui extended the anticolonial sentiment to the contemporary indigenous movement when he explained that the independent Latin American republics were formed "without and against" the original inhabitants. The anticolonial voice of the indigenous movement remains central to contemporary indigenous ideology.

The independent states in Latin America earnestly adopted the task of nation building from their European forefathers. As Latin American countries began to pursue nation building and a new "nationalist" discourse developed, it became clear that the Latin American elite considered extermination of the indigenous cultures to be necessary. They were convinced that "as long as indigenous peoples continued to constitute any substantial portion of the population, the Latin American countries would be unable to join the civilized nations of the world."[10]

In order to invent a national identity, then, indigenous heritage was appropriated as "folklore," and cultural costumes and music were brought into urban centers and displayed as the history and identity of the society, but always as something from the past. Indigenous people and their cultures were not integrated as equals into the new societies, which continue to have a European bias today. The myth of the unitary mestizo nation-state is the one that has been developed and still prevails in the Latin American nation-building process.

State-led attempts at building national hegemony throughout the region were unsuccessful in eradicating indigenous identity, although these initiatives did in some cases establish "campesino" in place of "Indian" as an organizational identity.[11] In general, the indigenous identity remains strongest in the periphery, where the new nation-state ideology permeated the least. The newly independent republics were, in effect, colonizing their own rural societies economically and culturally in order to build a nation.

The countries of Latin America remain ethnically diverse, although with arguably less violent ethnic antagonism than other regions. The major ethnic cleavages exist among the Spanish or Portuguese elite, the mestizo majority, and the indigenous and Afro-American minorities.[12] Ethnic political mobilization is common in the region, regardless of the size of the minority populations. In Latin America, it is useful to measure the success of nation building not against violent ethnic conflict but against social movements organized around ethnic identity. By that measure, countries with small minority indigenous populations, such as Colombia (2.2 percent) or Nicaragua (1.7 percent), have not succeeded at creating a strong homogeneous national identity; both Colombia and Nicaragua have politically active ethnonationalist indigenous and African-descent movements.[13]

Has nation building been successful in Latin America? Based on the vocabulary used by most political scientists regarding the region, it would seem so. The nation-state is the accepted unit of reference. Until very recently, social conflict outside party politics was discussed in terms of economic class, and popular opposition was measured in terms of the traditional political left. Even concerning countries with recent histories of violent conflicts, such as Guatemala or Peru, where indigenous people fill the ranks of guerrilla armies, political analyses have often skirted the underlying ethnic conflicts. However, it is my contention that the evidence shows that there are no unitary nation-states in Latin America, and ethnic cleavages continue to exist together with repression of indigenous rights. Nation building continues as a dominant paradigm, but the political expression of cultural diversity increasingly is encouraging a paradigm shift.

ETHNIC NATIONALISM IN POLITICAL ANALYSIS OF LATIN AMERICA

Despite the ethnic diversity in Latin America, until recently, U.S. political science on the region did not produce significant analysis of indigenous politics. Since the 1992 political mobilizations of indigenous people around the 500-year anniversary of the arrival of Christopher Columbus, political analysis of the movements has increased significantly.[14] A fundamental problem with most of the political science literature is that it is based on the assumption of a unified nation that in many cases actually is not consolidated. This problem can be seen in the discussions in the literature about building democracy in Latin America.

In his seminal article, "Transitions to Democracy," Dankwart Rustow laid the groundwork for many scholars who were trying to understand emerging democratic regimes in Latin America. Unlike most of the later publications, this article stresses the importance of national unity for a democracy. What is national unity? Rustow gives the following definition: "It simply means that the vast majority of citizens in a democracy-to-be must have no doubt or mental reservations as to which political community they belong."[15] Rustow highlights the relative importance of the issue to the process of democracy building, but his logic is flawed in that he describes national unity as a requirement for democracy. On the contrary, it is essential that a democracy reflect the ethnic diversity of a society. Why should the governing elite feel threatened in some cases and not in others while it is taking steps to share its power with a participatory civil society? My analysis shows that the threat is strongest when a popular movement is challenging the legitimacy of the nation itself. Let us consider some examples.

In Ecuador or Guatemala, where over half of the population is indigenous, a true democratic opening would entail extending democratic privileges of participation and access to a population that has been consistently excluded. Because of this exclusion,[16] indigenous communities consider the government to be a Spanish, or colonial, entity that does not represent them. Most of the leaders of popular indigenous groups in these two countries ask not for secession but for recognition of their rights as culturally distinct groups. Beyond that demand for special recognition, their demands resemble those of many other mobilized groups in civil society seeking, for example, the resolution of subsistence problems such as access to food and water. Despite their routine demands, indigenous movements are considered threatening, especially to a weak state lacking the capacity to reach rural areas and unable to meet those demands. Consequently, the political mobilization of large numbers of indigenous people can shatter the myth of a homogeneous nation-state.

In the case of the Miskito Indians on the Caribbean coast of Nicaragua, a group representing only 5 percent of the population threatened to divide the country with its demands for autonomy during the 1980s.[17] The Miskito had developed in relative isolation from the Spanish-speaking western side of the country, and most did not participate in the overthrow of the dictatorship of Anastasio Somoza. The Sandinista government at first did not consider them a threat. For most of the Miskito population, the Sandinista and the Somoza regimes were equally foreign. They had no attachment to the Nicaraguan state, the less so because half of the Miskito population lived across the river in Honduras. Sandinista policies, which did not take into account the ethnic diversity on the Caribbean coast, quickly alienated the indigenous populations; and the Miskito took up arms against the Sandinistas, with the backing of the United States. The Sandinista government was forced to make important concessions to the Miskito population, of which the most important was a law granting partial autonomy for the region's peoples.[18]

The Miskito case demonstrates how ethnicity can be mobilized against a political regime when the ethnic group has no loyalty to the government. The Sandinista regime was obliged to accept political policies that differed greatly from its socialist principles in order to incorporate the Miskito population into the nation of Nicaragua. The Sandinista government was weakened by the U.S.-backed Contra war, which increased the pressure to accept the Miskito's demands. The Miskito had the support of the United States, which led ethnic mobilization to become ethnic militancy. A similar case in Colombia supports this thesis but without the significant variable of external influences.

In Colombia, where a two-party coalition controls the government, the indigenous population accounts for only 3 percent of the total population and would probably be considered irrelevant in most circumstances. Yet, these indigenous people are so well organized that they have had more success than peasant organizations in obtaining land titles, and they also have been successful on a number of other political fronts — most recently, in electoral politics. At the beginning of the twenty-first century, with confidence in the ruling regime waning due to its inability to bring an end to Colombia's decades-old civil war, the indigenous population is actually growing because more peasants are openly recognizing their indigenous identity. Indigenous identity has become increasingly important in a country that has allowed practically no political participation by civil society outside of the two traditional parties. When elections for the 1991 Constitutional Assembly were held, allowing participation from outside the traditional parties for the first time since 1958, the indigenous groups won three seats in the Assembly, and, similarly, three permanent seats in Parliament for independent indigenous representatives. This demonstrates not only the indigenous groups' organizing skills, but also their popularity as an alternative and as a force for pluralism within the country.[19]

The Colombian and Nicaraguan cases are only two examples of the manner in which ethnic groups may organize under various types of regimes. Due to their unique relationship to the nation-state, indigenous groups can become particularly important when they mobilize, even when they are a minority. The concept of the resurrection of civil society is more complex when ethnicity is taken into account. Ethnic political mobilization can be considered as a method of resistance in exclusionary states. The potential influence of civil society in the democratization process is great.

DEMOCRACY AND MULTIETHNIC STATES

The democratic ideal implies a system to regulate internal group conflict.[20] For this reason, a regime in the process of building democratic
institutions should take up such a fundamental issue as ethnic diversity.
Instead, most of the literature concerning democracy in Latin America
implies that multiethnic countries cannot maintain a democratic society. Of
course, many countries — including Switzerland, Canada, and Great
Britain, among others — disprove that view.

My contention is that the issue of ethnic diversity should be reinte-
grated into debates about democratization. Given the recent intensification
of national divisions in Europe, such issues have begun to be addressed.
Although it is arguably more difficult to examine macro-variables such as
nationhood, it may be an analytical mistake to ignore them.

A pluri-national state can be considered a type of social contract in
which subgroups agree to sacrifice their autonomy in exchange for the
economic, social, and political benefits they receive from sharing a state.
The agreement can be entered into by force, by consent, by formal agreement, or tacitly. However, when the state becomes overtly loyal to one group
over another or when some groups' expectations are not met, these
marginalized groups may have cause to break the contract. The state has the
responsibility of providing an incentive for its member groups to remain
within the contract. The groups then have a responsibility to support the
functioning of the state. The problem with this model in Latin America is
that the weak nature of states and their poverty make it difficult for them to
meet their responsibilities to member groups, even in a democratic context.

Rustow's article, "Transitions to Democracy," is useful because of its
clarity on national unity. While I do not share the view that national unity is
a precondition for democracy, it is an important variable to consider. A more
accurate precondition for democracy is that a regime must demonstrate its
support equally to all the cultures in a society. Incorporation of this premise
will improve models of political development in Latin America and, beyond
that, will lead to a pluralistic type of democratic regime. The Latin American
regimes, as those elsewhere, can benefit from a model that guarantees the
government's loyalty to and support of different ethnic groups without
dividing citizenship.

POLITICIZED ETHNIC IDENTITY

The analysis of nation building that assumed the evolution of a homogeneous nation-state through economic development, which would then
lead to democracy, underestimated the transcendence of ethnic conflict in
this process. As Walker Connor points out, "The nation-building school

failed to give proper heed to what, in most states, was the major obstacle to political development."[21] Connor argues that scholars were too focused on the material incentives for differences within the nation; thus, they underestimated the emotional content of ethnic identity. This perspective is important to gain an understanding of the resilience of ethnic identity; however, to comprehend how it is transformed into a political movement, we need to examine how ethnic identity is used as a political resource.

Are social movements organized around ethnic identity representing political actors with strategies, or are they following their emotional connection to their ethnic roots?[22] The instrumentalist aspect of ethnic group mobilization contends that ethnicity can be used as a political tool to mobilize support for material or political gains. Some critics argue that this framework is overly materialist and undermines the true, emotive nature of ethnic identity. However, I argue that measurement of the success of a political movement, including an ethnic one, must include the material benefits that the movement can provide. Ethnic identity may, for example, provide access to certain government welfare programs. While it may be considered utilitarian to identify with an ethnic group to gain access to such a program, the fact that it is in an individual's interest to make the identification also provides evidence of the ethnic movement's success.

Political movements based on ethnic identity have not been eclipsed by class-based or electoral politics, as was previously expected. In the former Soviet bloc, the nationalist/secessionist movements of the 1980s undermined the goals of class-based unity. In Latin America, a dramatic resurgence in political mobilization is based on ethnic identification, both indigenous and Afro-American.

In Ecuador, the labor movement, which was strong in the 1970s, lost much of its momentum in the 1980s. Some argue that this is partly because of the failure of the left to adapt its ideology to the collapse of the Soviet Union. The indigenous movement, in contrast, has grown incrementally since that time and now has demonstrated that it can fill the streets more easily than the traditional labor federation, the United Workers Front (Frente Unido de Trabajadores — FUT).[23]

The class-based ideology behind the leftist movements in Latin America during the 1970s and 1980s directly influenced the political organizing of indigenous peoples. Indigenous groups were considered among the "oppressed masses" of Marxist-Leninist discourse. In some cases, indigenous peoples were involved in insurrectionary movements (Guatemala) or labor movements (Bolivia) or were used as political candidates for socialist parties (Ecuador and Colombia). Indigenous groups retained their ethnic allegiances, however, and in most cases formed independent organizations when the traditional left failed to support their cultural demands.

The alienation of the Miskito people from the Sandinista revolution in Nicaragua, discussed above, can be used to illustrate this point. Sandinista (that is, Marxist-Leninist) doctrine called for the rapid integration of traditional peoples into industrial society, to become a part of the popular classes organized by the self-described revolutionary government. Even when the Sandinistas agreed to a commendable policy of autonomy for indigenous people, it was limited: According to a report by one research institute, "There is a limit to how far the nation-state can give in to ethnically based demands for self-determination and autonomy without endangering its own claims to national sovereignty."[24]

In the Latin American context, governments are likely to consider ethnonationalist movements threatening to the sovereignty of the nation-state. Latin American countries have weak political institutions. In addition, contentious border issues still divide many Latin American countries. Indigenous demands often include claims over ancestral territory, and some government officials consider these a threat to economic security, as indigenous regions often are rich in natural resources. Earlier in this chapter, the point was made that indigenous identity is most cohesive in the periphery of Latin American nations, where ethnic identity is strongest. Because indigenous identity is strongest in the rural areas, where the state legitimacy is weakest , ethnonationalist movements based on indigenous identity are likely to be considered a national security threat by the state. Government authorities fear the indigenous challenge to the postcolonial order, including the possibilities of civil war or secession.

INDIGENOUS PERSPECTIVES

What is the indigenous perspective of the nation-state in Latin America? First and foremost, it is essential to recognize that indigenous people are actually hundreds of different diverse "peoples." Their relationship to each other is based on a shared social identity (as Indians), which came after generations of colonization. Within each indigenous culture is a further diversity in levels of isolation and education, vocation, relationship to the political system, and so on. Accordingly, no single indigenous perspective exists. In the past 20 years, more indigenous people have written about their own perspectives on the indigenous experience in Latin America, including indigenous identity and politics. We can ascertain some commonalties of the indigenous perspective on the nation-state and of the contemporary indigenous political movement. The areas where various indigenous perspectives include commonalties despite differences can be regarded as a contemporary indigenous ideology.

All indigenous peoples share the common heritage of the European conquest, which for them was genocide. With that history comes a perspective of Europeans as oppressors. The indigenous population on the continent is widely considered to have decreased by 80 percent (from around 100 million) in the first 50 years after European contact. As Rodolfo Stavenhagen has asserted, "By today's standards, this would be labeled genocide, and it is considered such by indigenous organizations of the continent."[25]

The centrality of European conquest to indigenous ideology explains the important factor that contemporary indigenous identity is based on "the other," a factor that indigenous organizations continue to promote in their counter-hegemonic discourse. Numerous anthropologists have noted this. For example, Janet Hendricks has observed, "Perhaps the most important factor of the (Shuar) Federation's success is its role in reinforcing and recreating a sense of Shuar identity based on egalitarianism and hostility toward outsiders, and the belief system that supports these principles."[26]

The contemporary indigenous ideology was developed in the context of nation-building strategies by the state. As a result, indigenous people often claim to see themselves as outside the nation and separate from its citizenship. Indigenous leaders of the 1970s adopted the term "nationalities," the same term that was being used in the Soviet Union to describe the ethnically different nations within its confederation. According to Iliana Almeida, an anthropologist close to the movement in Ecuador, the concept of nationalities was brought back from the Soviet Union by sympathizers who were allies of the fledgling indigenous organizations.[27] Recognition by the government as nationalities could allow indigenous groups to claim entitlement to special rights.

Contemporary ethnonationalist movements are unique in that they develop in a world of nation-states that have accepted the juridical concept that not only individuals, but also "peoples" have rights. The post-World War II accords on human rights set forth in the Geneva Convention recognize the rights of peoples. Moreover, the United Nations International Convention on Economic, Social, and Cultural Rights recognizes group rights, such as the right to a healthy environment, which are especially important to indigenous peoples. The International Labor Organization (ILO), part of the United Nations system, sponsored ILO Convention 169, an international covenant that recognizes many specific rights of indigenous peoples. Most of the literature on nation-states and nationalism does not take into account this new context of human rights. Thus, this body of literature fails to express the political influence of "autonomy" movements in contemporary multiethnic countries.

The indigenous movement in the Americas, particularly in Ecuador, has been influenced by the growing vernacular concerning the rights of peoples. For the indigenous movement, whose members have been excluded economically and politically from the nation-state system, the "rights of peoples" is a rallying point. Hundreds of indigenous activists have traveled to testify at the annual Human Rights Convention in Geneva, and thousands have participated in the International Working Group on the Rights of Indigenous Peoples. They argue that they are one-tenth of Latin America's population, approximately 35 million people, yet they are not represented in the United Nations. The UN venue has given indigenous peoples the language of human rights and has provided them a stage for challenging governments in a setting that legitimizes their civil rights.

In almost all cases, Latin American indigenous organizations are not secessionist; that is, they are not demanding their own states. Instead, they are claiming the right to various degrees of political, economic, and cultural autonomy. Their claims include respect for customary law, so that they may implement their traditional justice systems in their own communities (for which there is legal precedent in international law) and the guarantee of territorial bases, so that they can nurture and reproduce their unique cultures.

NATION-STATE IN ECUADOR

Ecuador fits the model of an unfinished nation. There is a sense of patriotism in the country, especially around elections and border disputes; however, the urban and rural poor generally consider themselves abandoned by the government, and a substantial percentage of the indigenous people question the legitimacy of a Hispanic state that does not represent them. The political institutions of the democratic system are weak in the countryside, with the traditional patron-client politics of bartering political power for economic favors.

The indigenous movement represents an ethnic cleavage group that challenges the Ecuadoran nation-state. The indigenous movement's strong political mobilizations in recent decades bring into question the current nation-building model. Indigenous leaders in Ecuador demanded that the Ecuadoran Constitution be modified to recognize the country as a "plurinational state." They refer to their collective groups as "nationalities," signifying that they were nations before the conquest but not necessarily implying that they are in pursuit of their own state. Still, these concepts make the Ecuadoran governing class uncomfortable. In an interview, an Ecuadoran provincial authority offered this perspective on indigenous people: "They are wrong to call themselves nationalities. . . . We do not want to have one nation here, another there, divided amongst ourselves."[28]

CONCLUSIONS

The indigenous movement in Latin America is the contemporary expression of the clash of cultures that began 500 years ago. To date, discussions of nationalism and ethnic conflict consider ethnic diversity to be an impediment to democracy. From this perspective, a contradiction exists between ethnonationalism and nation building that can lead to ethnic conflict. Prevailing development ideology calls for a homogeneous national culture that somehow manages to establish culturally uniform democratic institutions. Political exclusion and/or homogenization of competing ethnic identities preserve this cultural divide. An alternate perspective could be considered, based on a democratic government's ability to rectify this cultural clash. I believe that further study will indicate that the demands placed on the state by ethnic mobilization provide opportunities for expanding democracy — if governments were to respond by being open to increased indigenous participation. Thus, governments would strengthen their legitimacy in the eyes of all citizens.

In Ecuador, the indigenous political movement has asserted its right to inclusion and equal participation in the Ecuadoran nation. Ethnic allegiance and national citizenship need not be mutually exclusive. In fact, democratic nation building is enhanced when governments maintain loyalty to more than one ethnic group. Inclusive political action expands a government's legitimacy and strengthens the institutional decision-making processes necessary for a participatory democratic system.

The Constitution now recognizes Ecuador's cultural diversity.

Notes

1. Anthony Smith, 1993, *National Identity* (Reno: University of Nevada Press), 14.

2. Alison Brysk describes the influence of the United Nations (UN) Human Rights regime on indigenous movements. See Brysk 2000.

3. Benedict Anderson, 1983, *Imagined Communities: Reflections on the Origins and Spread of Nationalism* (London: Verso).

4. This definition borrows from the work of Anthony Smith, 1971, *Theories of Nationalism* (London: Duckworth).

5. Alexander Motyl has argued, along the lines of Ernest Gellner, that the nationalist movement is inherently "modern," in that it is concerned with the control of the state, a modern phenomenon. This works within his paradigm of nationalism, which, as John Breuilly also described it, aims at capturing the modern state. I suggest that an ethnonationalist movement, such as an indigenous movement, may not have a separatist ideology. See Alexander Motyl, 1992, "The Modernity of Nationalism," *Journal of International Affairs* 45 (2): 307-323; Ernest Gellner, 1983, *Nations and Nationalism* (Ithaca, N.Y.: Cornell University Press); and John Breuilly, 1985, *Nationalism and the State* (Manchester, U.K.: Manchester University Press).

6. See Kotkin, 1992, *Tribes* (New York: Random House), for a discussion of supra-national ethnic ties in the modern market.

7. Anthony Smith, 1986, "State-making and Nation-building," in *States in History*, ed. John Hall (Oxford: Blackwell), 1.

8. The central scholars in the field, such as Ernest Gellner, Benedict Anderson, Anthony Smith, and E. J. Hobsbawm make almost no reference to Latin America.

9. In fact, the Miskito in Nicaragua, the Quintín Lame guerrilla movement in Colombia, and the Zapatistas in Mexico provide a few examples of organized ethnic revolt in modern Latin America; however, compared to other regions, ethnic violence in Ecuador has been relatively unthreatening.

10. Rodolfo Stavenhagen, 1992, "Challenging the Nation State in Latin America," *Journal of International Affairs* 45 (2): 426.

11. See Florencia Mallon, 1992, "Indian Communities, Political Cultures, and the State in Latin America, 1780-1990," *Journal of Latin American Studies* 24 (Quincentenary Supplement 1992), for a summary of these processes in Bolivia, Peru, and Mexico.

12. See Peter Wade, 1997, *Race and Ethnicity in Latin America* (Chicago: Pluto Press), for discussion of race and ethnic identity in Latin America. For my purposes, ethnicity is a more fluid identification than race, and it concerns culture and shared history. Race is a more biologically determined characteristic. Ethnicity, for example, may not be determined by appearance. African origin has both an ethnic and a racial aspect.

13. The rest of the populations are diverse. Colombia has a vociferous Afro-Colombian movement that includes about 26 percent of the population. People of African descent have special rights under the Colombian and Nicaraguan constitutions (I am grateful to Jonathan Fox for pointing this out).

14. Deborah Yashar, Alison Brysk, and Donna Van Cott make important contributions to this subject in their work.

15. Rustow 1970, 350.

16. I use the term "exclusion" here as a rough translation for the Spanish concept of *marginalización*.

17. For a complete discussion of the "national question" in Nicaragua, see the detailed account in Hale 1994. This analysis also is based on my field research in 1986.

18. For simplicity, I mention only the Miskito here, but it is important to note that the region is inhabited by Sumu, Rama, Garífuna, and Creole populations as well; all of whom participated in ethnic mobilizations.

19. This analysis is from my own field research in Colombia during June-September 1990.

20. Adam Przeworski, 1988, "Some Problems in the Study of the Transition to Democracy," in *Transitions from Authoritarian Rule: Comparative Perspectives*, eds. Guillermo O'Donnell, Philippe C. Schmitter, and Laurence Whitehead (Baltimore: The Johns Hopkins University Press), 47-64.

21. Walker Connor, 1987, "Ethnonationalism," in *Understanding Political Development: An Analytic Study*, eds. Myron Weiner and Samuel P. Huntington (Boston: Little, Brown), 199.

22. This emotional description of ethnic ties is often referred to as "primordialist."

23. Most of the analysis of the 1990 Indigenous Uprising confirms this fact. The United Federation of Workers represents the three largest trade union federations and is the most important workers' organization in the country.

24. CIDCA (Centro de Información y Documentación de la Costa Atlántica), 1987, *Ethnic Groups and the Nation-State: The Case of the Atlantic Coast in Nicaragua* (Stockholm: University of Stockholm). Also, see Hale 1994 for a lengthy discussion of class and ethnicity in Nicaragua.

25. Stavenhagen 1992, 424.

26. Janet Hendricks, 1991, "Symbolic Counterhegemony among the Ecuadoran Shuar," in *Nation-States and Indians in Latin America,* eds. Greg Urban and Steven Scherzer (Austin, Texas: University of Texas Press), 57.

27. Iliana Almeida, anthropologist, 1991, interview by author.

28. Fausto Espín, governor of Pastaza province, 1993, interview by author.

Chapter 3

Indigenous-State Relations in Ecuador: The Politics of Culture

INTRODUCTION

What it means to be indigenous in Ecuador has changed over the last two decades, as indigenous organizations have emerged to present a new image. Concurrently, government policy has changed with each administration in a gradual shift from exclusion of indigenous people toward attempts to include them in the political system. As discussed in Chapter 2, the Ecuadoran nation can be considered "unfinished" to the extent that the government endeavors to build a unified nation-state political model. The Hispanic political culture still dominates and excludes the majority of the indigenous population from adequate participation in decisionmaking and benefit sharing. Ecuador's case illustrates how the cultural identity of a group can be significant in the political arena. The nation-building paradigm, which calls for a unified culture, requires indigenous people to sacrifice their identity in order to benefit from the social contract of the polity. Their exclusion, while partially influenced by class and geography, is based primarily on their identification with a premodern social system considered by Ecuador's political intelligentsia to be antithetical to the contemporary nation-state.

This chapter presents an account of the changing relationship between the government and the indigenous movement, focusing on the period from the return to electoral democracy with the election of Roldós in 1979 through the administration of Durán Ballén, ending in 1996. During this period, the new indigenous ideology emerged, and the Confederation of Indigenous Nationalities of Ecuador (CONAIE) was consolidated as Ecuador's most important indigenous organization. The indigenous organizations made a formal decision to support indigenous participation in electoral politics in 1996, a move that brought them into a new period of indigenous politics. These developments substantiate my contention that Ecuador's indigenous people have pushed for democratic reforms leading to a participatory, multiethnic political system.

This chapter also outlines the indigenous movement's evolution from distinct socioeconomic groupings throughout the country into a relatively unified organized movement. It then describes the policies of the various administrations toward the indigenous question. The analysis of the relationship between the social movement and the government's response to it describes the context in which cultural demands have led to greater political openings for the indigenous people in Ecuador.

The leaders of the indigenous movement have created a political space for the indigenous population by making "cultural" demands on the political system. These demands, for example, for the right to bilingual education, have received more response from the government than the movement's territorial demands, which were considered linked to traditional leftist, class-based political movements. Through its cultural battles, and, in particular, through bilingual education, the indigenous movement has created a strong organizational base that now plays a leading role in the national political scene.

Through its search to define a political voice in a context of exclusion, the indigenous population has become one of Ecuador's most significant social movements. While labor-based movements declined in membership during the 1980s, indigenous organizations demonstrated an increasing ability to mobilize massive protests. Demonstrations against the Durán administration's economic liberalization policies, for example, arguably succeeded only because of indigenous participation. A 1992 strike by Social Security Department workers was hardly noticed for a week, until the rural sector joined the protests — at which point a resolution was reached within a few days. Similarly, a strike called by the important FUT for May Day 1993, was insignificant, but when the FUT had the support of indigenous organizations a few weeks later to protest government economic reforms, the entire country was affected.[1] A newspaper editorial suggested, "The cause of the indigenous people has the support of the population, but that is not true for the FUT leaders."[2]

The indigenous movement has demonstrated its success in a number of other ways. A common method of measuring the success of a movement is by noting its ability to convoke mass protests as a measure of its popularity. The indigenous movement has demonstrated that resistance can and does take place on a variety of other levels that are less easily observed.[3] In the case of the indigenous movement, when its members are not in the streets, they are engaged in reinventing indigenous identity through bilingual education and through organizing in indigenous communities. As this chapter demonstrates, the movement has won a place on the political agenda, so that indigenous people are increasingly active participants in Ecuadoran civil society.

The following section of this chapter traces how the government and the indigenous movement developed in relation to one another during the

1979-1986 period. Organizational experiences of indigenous communities in the Amazon and the Sierra (the Andean Highlands) will be outlined, including the issues they have confronted and the political process of their forming a national organization. A brief description of past governments' policies toward the indigenous groups will follow. As the movement's history during these important years is described, it becomes clear that the cultural demands of the indigenous movement in Ecuador allowed it to reinvent indigenous identity and create a significant political force that surprised both the left and the government.

Rafael Pandam, Shuar representative at CONAIE assembly in August 1991.

INDIGENOUS ORGANIZATIONS

The indigenous movement in Ecuador has a long history, or rather, two very distinct histories: that of the Sierra and that of the Amazon region. Out of these very different experiences grew the national federation structure that quickly moved to the forefront of the Ecuadoran indigenous movement, CONAIE.

The historical context of indigenous politics in Ecuador is rooted in the colonial system of racial division that Andrés Guerrero aptly calls "ethnic administration."[4] The Spanish conquest of the Andean region and wars with the Inca empire devastated the indigenous populations of the region, began the process of enslavement and acculturation, and set the stage for Spanish domination. Economic and social segregation kept the indigenous populations on the periphery of mainstream development. By the time of the first agrarian reform in 1964, a large indigenous population still was excluded from political and economic power in Ecuador.

It is important to underline the relationship between the indigenous movement and the left because of the Cold War perspective that persists in Latin America, in which popular opposition to the government often is considered linked to communism. A broad spectrum of political ideologies can be found within the indigenous movement. In some cases, indigenous groups have actively rejected the left and allied themselves with conservative political sectors.[5] In Ecuador, this trend is most evident in communities influenced by conservative Protestant missionaries. Simultaneously, many indigenous intellectuals were inspired in the early 1970s by socialist struggles such as that of Salvador Allende in Chile and the Cuban Revolution. In the words of Humberto Muenala,

"Maybe we weren't members, but we were sympathizers, helpers of the Socialist movement. What with everything that was happening with Allende in Chile . . . we were the ones who translated what they wanted to say in the indigenous communities, and when we began to talk about our own proposals, like indigenous education, they started to get angry."[6]

The indigenous movement, as well as other new social movements, engages in forms of social protest that do not necessarily fit into traditional schemes of left-right politics.[7]

AMAZON ORGANIZATIONS

Indigenous communities in the Amazon have been the least acculturated, despite their constant confrontations with missionaries, colonization, and oil and other extractive industries. Their relative geographic isolation has ensured greater cultural coherence; also, they were less targeted by government policies of assimilation than the indigenous people of the Coast and the Highlands. Education, for example, was controlled by missionary groups, such as the Summer Institute of Linguistics, which often encouraged education in native languages, as compared with government schools in the Sierra that imposed Spanish.

Agrarian reform laws in Ecuador dramatically affected the Amazon. A military junta passed the first Agrarian Reform Law in 1964. The law created the Ecuadoran Institute for Agrarian Reform and Colonization (Instituto Ecuatoriano de Reforma Agraria y Colonización — IERAC), which actively promoted the colonization of the Amazon as a way to relieve pressure for arable land in the Sierra. Land hitherto used by indigenous communities was claimed by settlers, mestizos, and indigenous groups from the Highlands, who were granted land titles by the government when they cleared the land and began agricultural production on it. An oil boom in the early 1970s intensified colonization and had devastating impacts on the ecology and the way of life in the upper Amazonian region.

One of the first contemporary indigenous organizations in Ecuador was the Federation of Shuar Centers (Federación de Centros Shuar), established in 1964. Ironically, the federation originally was formed with the aid of Salesian missionaries who had established control in the Shuar territory and were apprehensive about losing their hold due to accelerated colonization. The federation has succeeded in securing most of the indigenous territory in the form of communal "center" or "community" holdings. Besides the immediate need to consolidate landholdings, the federation has the long-term goal of ensuring the survival of Shuar culture. The federation has developed successful bilingual education and health programs that have given it some independence from Ecuadoran government programs.

The federation has come under scrutiny recently, however, because the economic stability of the Shuar is based primarily on cattle ranching, an enterprise that is considered damaging to the sensitive rain-forest environment and to traditional indigenous agriculture. Despite long-standing disputes between the Shuar and other peoples of the Amazon, the Shuar participate in regional and national indigenous organizations, and their federation has served as a political model for other organizations throughout the country.

Provincial organizations began to form throughout the Amazon during the 1970s in response to the threat to indigenous land and culture from colonization. The Organization of Indigenous Peoples of Pastaza (Organización de Pueblos Indígenas de Pastaza — OPIP), the Federation of Indigenous Organizations of Napo (Federación de Organizaciones Indígenas de Napo — FOIN), and others were formed to act as a political voice in the many land conflicts. These federations mixed traditional methods of community organization, such as shamanism (with traditional medicine men and "chiefs"), together with a Western model of organizational structure (that is, including a president, vice-president, secretary, and so on). The organizations were formed with the clear goal of cultural survival, but the concrete political struggles were over land — the core of indigenous existence.

When the various local groups began to work together, they decided to unite the various Amazon organizations; and in 1980 the Confederation of Indigenous Nationalities of the Ecuadoran Amazon (Confederación de Nacionalidades Indígenas de la Amazonia Ecuatoriana — CONFENIAE) emerged. CONFENIAE is now a well-structured organization with a large base near the Amazon frontier town of Puyo. The goal was to organize delegates from each indigenous nation, as opposed to the national administrative divisions. The leadership of CONFENIAE has been mostly Shuar and Quichua, although the other, smaller nationalities of the Amazon — Achuar, Huaorani, Cofán, Siona, and Secoya — are active participants. It is particularly important that these small nationalities are involved because they are nearly extinct, due to infrastructure development and oil extraction in their traditional territories. Whereas 25 years ago each nationality comprised about 20,000 people, their numbers have dwindled to between 700 and 1,200 individuals in each group. The main decision-making body of this confederation is the Congress, which meets every two years. At each Congress, participants analyze the present state of events, make policy and strategic decisions, and elect the directive committee for the next two-year period.

CONFENIAE ushered in a new era for the indigenous people of the Amazon, bringing their issues onto the political agenda in an organized manner. The Confederation formed alliances with politicians and with human rights and environmental activists. Through these alliances, oil companies and the government were brought to the negotiating table, particularly regarding the issue of development practices in the Amazon; moreover, according to some observers, CONFENIAE has begun to make a dent in conservation strategies for oil extraction in the region. It also assisted in obtaining communal titles to large tracts of land for the Huaorani people and for the Quichua of Pastaza, organized by OPIP.

The territory granted to OPIP is of particular significance because it represents the largest communal land title in the Amazon. The title was granted after a massive march of Quichua people from the Amazon to the capital city of Quito in April 1992. A source from within the government asserts that the territory was likely to have been given to the Quichua even without their protest. The OPIP insists, however, that the presence of 3,000 indigenous people camping out in a public park in the capital pressured the government into granting the title. In any case, the government's act was a public recognition of the right of the indigenous peoples of the Amazon to land. Concurrently, the march demonstrated the indigenous federations' high level of organization and the tremendous amount of public support for their cause. Indigenous and other groups that offered food and supplies, as well as moral support, met the marchers along the road to Quito.

The environmental sector is one of the most important allies of the indigenous peoples of the Amazon. Both internationally and within Ecuador, many ecologists have come to recognize that the native people of the Amazon are important defenders of the ecosystem, and some environmental groups now actively support the indigenous federations. Previously, environmental groups often ignored indigenous people, and some of the resulting animosity remains. For example, conservation groups brokered debt-for-nature swaps in which Latin American governments set up protected areas in exchange for a portion of their external debt. These agreements were made without consulting the indigenous people who lived there, and in some cases the agreements led to their relocation. Increasingly, environmental groups now are considered allies.

The Amazon federations were formed with a clear identity focus because they were organized against the primarily nonindigenous settlers and because their geographic isolation left them with a stronger sense of separate identity than that of indigenous groups in the Sierra. To this day, resentment and difficulty often surface in organizing among indigenous groups from the two regions. Still, as described below, the Sierra groups joined with the Amazon groups to create the national political space that the indigenous movement now occupies.

HIGHLANDS ORGANIZATIONS

Contemporary forms of indigenous organizations in the Highlands, or Sierra, have their roots in the agrarian reform process that began in Ecuador in the 1960s, but indigenous resistance has persisted since the Spanish conquest, and rebellions continued throughout the colonial and republican periods. Despite periodic uprisings by indigenous communities, nonindigenous society has considered them submissive, and that is the common image used to portray indigenous people in Ecuador. Another common conception is that the indigenous peoples are "backward" and, therefore, are holding the country back economically and politically. Perhaps the most important triumph of the indigenous organizations thus far is that they have successfully challenged those stereotypes.

One of the earliest indigenous organizations in the Sierra was the Indigenous Federation of Ecuador (Federación Ecuatoriana de Indígenas — FEI). Members of the Ecuadoran Communist Party who saw the need to establish a peasant organization formed the FEI in 1944 in the first national attempt to organize indigenous rural workers. The FEI intended to organize the indigenous communities as laborers, rather than as indentured peasants, and to push for a land reform that would lead to redistribution of agrarian wealth. Scores of protests and land takeovers were sponsored by the FEI, and some cite these protests as an incentive for the Agrarian Reform Law.

The Agrarian Reform Law of 1964 is considered by analysts to be a turning point in indigenous politics because it radically changed the social structure of rural Ecuador. The debt-peonage farm system (*huasipungo*), Ecuador's version of indentured agricultural labor (service tenure), was outlawed. However, while workers were freed from unpaid labor, they lost access to the hacienda owners' pastures and forests. Some argue that the agrarian laborers, mostly indigenous, suffered economically because they lost access to land they had used for subsistence farming. At the same time, the reform initiated dramatic growth in indigenous organizing.

Indigenous communities organized chiefly around land conflicts to demand land that they considered to be unjustly in the hands of large property owners. Also, increasing numbers of communities began to organize as *comunas*, or agricultural communities, in accordance with the Ley de Comunas of 1936. This law, which did not apply to *huasipungeros* (share-croppers), allows for a community to organize its own official local government, a community council called a *cabildo*, and promises a limited degree of autonomy over natural resources and government support for community development. Since that time, the cabildos became increasingly important in the development of indigenous organizations in the Sierra. A community had to be organized and registered in order to make a land claim to the government. Between 1974 and 1990, the number of indigenous communities registered as comunas or other types of associations grew from 1,530 to 2,236.[8]

Religious influences have been very strong in indigenous organizing in the Highlands, particularly in the central region. The Roman Catholic Church reacted to the FEI's efforts by working to promote a noncommunist-affiliated organization. The church sponsored a regional meeting of local organizations from which the regional organization of Quichua peoples (Confederación de Pueblos de la Nacionalidad Quichua del Ecuador — ECUARUNARI, also called *Ecuador Runacunapac Riccharimui* — Ecuador Indians Awaken), emerged in 1972.

ECUARUNARI has undergone major ideological shifts over the years, as shown by records of the organization's annual Congresses. At the first Congress, for example, ECUARUNARI was declared an ecclesiastical organization, with a priest as an advisor to teach principles of organization and to encourage rejection of communist involvement. Later documents recorded that the organization questioned the role of the church and called for unity between the struggles of indigenous peoples and workers.[9] Other records show that some members went as far as advocating "struggle for the formation of a socialist state."[10]

Ideological debates have continued among the organization's leadership, but the image ECUARUNARI promotes is one of an identity-based

CONAIE supports agrarian cooperatives like this one in Imbabura.

organization that nonetheless calls for unity between indigenous groups and peasants. While ECUARUNARI still emphasizes the resolution of land conflicts, it played an important role in organizing the international "500 Years of Indigenous Resistance" campaigns during 1990, 1991, and 1992. ECUARUNARI functions as a federation of local organizations for the Highlands in much the same way that CONFENIAE does for the Amazon, with regular congresses and a directive committee.

NATIONAL ORGANIZATIONS

CONAIE is the internationally recognized national organization representing the indigenous people of Ecuador. Formed in 1980 by the leadership of CONFENIAE and ECUARUNARI to act as a coordinating body for the indigenous organizations, it quickly took on a political life of its own. At its formation, when it was a coordinating body called the Coordinating Council of Indigenous Nationalities of Ecuador (Consejo de Coordinación Nacional de las Naciones Indígenas — CONACNIE), the national organization aimed to unite the diverse regional demands into a unified national indigenous movement. The Highlands' organizations were focused almost exclusively on land recuperation, while the Amazon's organizations became involved with the impacts of development, including colonization and environmental issues. In addition to regional specificity, ideological differences and debates about class and ethnicity were found within the movement.

The primary responsibility of CONACNIE was to lead the movement toward unity. As a spokesperson for the movement explained, "Although each organization has achieved its own success, we are aware that the unity of all the indigenous people is indispensable for our movement to have the necessary force to achieve economic, social, cultural, and political objectives."[11] In addition, the temporary organization was to organize a second national meeting in 1984. The resolutions of the first (1980) encounter included commitments to strengthen the local organizations and to support bilingual education and the development of leaders. One of the most important objectives that emerged from the first encounter was to reject the "paternalism and manipulation" of political parties, missionaries, and other groups or institutions. So, an important founding principle of the national organization was independence from other social sectors. At the same time, resolutions from the first meeting expressed a commitment to maintain relationships with class-based and international organizations when they represent similar interests.

In its six years of existence as CONACNIE, the national organization began to represent the interests of all the indigenous groups. Among other achievements, two are especially notable for our discussion. First, CONACNIE convinced the national civil registry to accept indigenous-language names for the first time in history. Second, it helped force the Summer Institute of Linguistics, a conservative missionary organization, to leave the country. The roots of the new indigenous ideology can be seen clearly in these actions. In addition, both actions affected the daily lives of Ecuador's indigenous people, promoting the usefulness of a national organization.

CONAIE has functioned as the national organization since its establishment at a second indigenous General Assembly in 1986. Along with CONFENIAE and ECUARUNARI, a coastal organization was also formed, the Coordinator of Indigenous Organizations of the Coast of Ecuador (Coordinadora de Organizaciones de la Costa Ecuatoriana — COICE) so that the three regional areas of Ecuador could be represented through CONAIE. Delegates from the entire country meet every two to three years for a CONAIE Congress to evaluate the movement and elect new leadership. The organization's leadership structure has changed over the years to include a president, vice president, secretary of organization and promotion, secretary of human rights, secretary of women, secretary of health, and secretary of education. CONAIE's permanent office is in Quito, where the organization is based; however, its elected leaders travel around the country, and assemblies and congresses are held at various locations around the country. The first few years of CONAIE's existence were spent trying to "establish itself as an organization, balance the representation of the Sierra and Amazon, gain access to resources, and establish the infrastructure necessary to guarantee its functioning."[12]

CONAIE works to promote indigenous rights in all areas. It has a number of supporters, from environmentalists to anthropologists, as well as international economic benefactors. Institutional supporters from the United States include OXFAM America,[13] the Inter-American Foundation, and the Rainforest Action Network. Together with these allies and the dedication of indigenous community leaders, CONAIE leads what has become the most prominent social movement in the country. The organization has both immediate and long-term goals. The most immediate objective remains the resolution of land conflicts in the Highlands and territorial disputes in the Amazon. At the same time, more far-reaching political goals have emerged, such as the controversial demand to reform the Constitution and recognize Ecuador as a "pluri-national state." In the constitutional reforms of 1998, Ecuador declared itself a pluri-national state.

Clearly, the event that established the legitimacy of CONAIE was the Indigenous Uprising of June 1990. After weeks of organizing and frustrated by stagnating talks with the government, CONAIE called for an uprising that nearly paralyzed the country for more than a week. Main access roads were blocked; markets were boycotted; water supplies to urban areas were cut off; and, in some cases, military personnel were kidnapped and held hostage by indigenous groups. The hostages were released unharmed after local government officials signed an agreement with CONAIE promising to respond to its demands. The 1990 Uprising[14] shattered the stereotype of the passive "humble Indian" and established a political presence for CONAIE.

A plethora of literature has sprung up since the 1990 Uprising, discussing the Indian/indigenous movement and its origins from differing perspectives.[15] There is unanimous agreement that the situation has changed since the 1990 Uprising: "Whether elevated or lowered, admired or misunderstood, idealized or banalized, the Indians have returned to the Ecuadoran conscience, and it is no longer possible to imagine a destiny together without considering their presence and participation."[16]

The 1990 Uprising brought to the surface many fears, tensions, and criticisms within Ecuadoran society about the growth of the indigenous movement. For instance, one agricultural analyst asked,

"Who is going to think of investing in the countryside when, along with the lack of security and stimulus to invest, there is now a new phantom, that of the indigenous nationalities who destroy our mestizo ethnic unity and try to nullify white, black, and mestizo participation in the development of our countryside . . .?[17]

These fears, particularly about the potential division of the mestizo nation, continue to stimulate opposition to the indigenous movement and to CONAIE in particular.

CONAIE further established itself as a central representative of indigenous people when the Rodrigo Borja administration (1988-1992) granted the organization a large degree of control over the bilingual education program. Bilingual, bicultural education has been one of the most important factors in the indigenous movement in Ecuador for a number of reasons. First, it was a primary point of contention between classist-influenced indigenous leaders, who saw it as bourgeois, and ethnicity-based leaders, who saw it as a basic need of indigenous people. Some indigenous leaders suggested that a political focus on cultural issues, such as language, detracted from their immediate struggle for land. The traditional leftist organizations believed language retention would divide the working class, so at first they did not support the call for bilingual education, although later they did support it.[18]

Government acceptance of the Quichua language reflects changing perceptions of indigenous society as a whole and institutionalizes the favorable status of a language that was considered on the verge of disappearance, a language that people resisted speaking until a few years ago because it was so scorned. Most important, bilingual literacy campaigns and education have contributed to the reinvention of indigenous identity in Ecuador and have provided the basis for the success of CONAIE.[19]

CONAIE has consistently challenged the neoliberal economic policies that began to dominate Latin American politics during the 1980s. As José Almeida argues, "The indigenous proposal demands that the state change to incorporate the political advances in the popular sectors, and to protect the production conditions and social life of the indigenous people as they face the voracity of 'neo-liberalism.'"[20]

CONAIE has not been alone in encouraging the resurgence of indigenous identity and criticizing neoliberal economic policies. A few other indigenous organizations should also be taken into consideration, for example, the Federation of Indigenous Evangelicals (Federación Ecuatoriana de Indígenas Evangélicos — FEINE), a well-financed group that is strongest in the central Sierra, around Chimborazo. This group's benefactors are primarily fundamentalist Christian groups from the United States that have been sending increasing numbers of missionaries to Latin America. These missionaries tend to be politically conservative, and some have actively denounced CONAIE. However, the relationship between the evangelical groups and CONAIE began to improve in the early 1990s, as indigenous groups forged increased unity. In the central province of Bolívar, for example, Juan Arévalo, an Indian leader who converted to evangelical

Christianity, was elected president of a CONAIE affiliate, the Bolívar Campesino Federation (Federación Campesina de Bolívar — FECAB). Arévalo has said his political values have remained the same since his pre-evangelical days; one behavioral change he has made is that he no longer drinks alcohol.[21]

Another important national organization is the National Federation of Campesino Organizations (Federación Nacional de Organizaciones Campesinas — FENOC), a labor-based group formed in 1944. This alliance changed its name to the National Federation of Campesino and Indigenous Organizations (Federación Nacional de Organizaciones Campesinas e Indígenas — FENOC-I): the 'I' stands for "indigenous," although most people still refer to it by its original name. More recently, this organization changed its name again to the National Federation of Campesinos, Indigenous, and Negro Organizations (Federación Nacional de Organizaciones Campesinas, Indígenas, y Negras — FENOCIN). Although this group appears more influential than CONAIE in the canton of Cotocachi, where FENOCIN's headquarters and support base are located, it has failed to establish a strong national presence. FENOC was developed in the context of land conflicts and had a platform similar to that of the early ECUARUNARI: "putting all of the emphasis on the struggle for land, and paying little attention to ethnic considerations."[22] Members of both organizations have said they believe the movement as a whole is strengthened by a plurality of voices, although they often express their distrust of each other.[23] However, they have united to take certain actions with regard to the national government, for example, cooperation in the 1990 Uprising and joint support of specific indigenous law projects.

GOVERNMENT POLICY

Latin American governments have applied different strategies through the years to deal with indigenous populations, but they continue to work within the same overall constraints. The Ecuadoran state has taken up the challenge of developing a strong nation to compete economically and politically in a world of nation-states. Essentially a "developmentalist" state, Ecuador is focused on a model of rapid industrial development to spur the economic growth necessary to solve the country's social problems. As noted in Chapter 2, the government can find itself in a contradictory position in reference to the indigenous population. In the first place, the state has undertaken a democratic project, which entails developing a society that respects all the liberal concepts of a democracy, including pluralism. At the same time, most government policy actually is based on "modernization" as an objective, a project that involves the creation of a strong national identity and the acculturation of indigenous peoples into the dominant social and economic culture.

During interviews for this study, a number of local and even provincial government authorities expressed the view without hesitation that the main reason Ecuador is so poor is that "it has so many Indians." No authorities at the national level stated these positions openly, so perhaps this perspective is changing. Clearly, policies regarding indigenous people in Ecuador are changing at all levels, from a completely exclusionary policy to a variety of attempts at inclusion, including some specific legislation. The following analysis of government policy toward the indigenous sector will begin with the election of President Roldós after a period of military rule, because the time after his election was significant for the integration of indigenous people into national politics.

Roldós Administration

The election of Jaime Roldós of the Concentration of Popular Forces Party (Concentración de Fuerzas Populares — CFP), as president in 1979 saw a return to institutional democracy in Ecuador, with the end of military rule and the defeat of a more conservative candidate backed by the military (Sixto Durán Ballén, who was elected as president from 1992 to 1996). In his campaign, Roldós presented himself as the "people's president" and solicited the votes of the poor, particularly the illiterate, who were voting for the first time as a result of constitutional reforms. Most of the illiterate population was indigenous, so this meant initiation of that group into electoral politics.

The Roldós administration promoted bilingual education in the country, most important, through an accord between the Ministry of Education and Culture and the Center for the Investigation of Indigenous Education (Centro de Investigaciones para la Educación Indígena — CIEI) at the Catholic University. The Center promoted the first systematic study of bilingual education and adult literacy projects at the national level. CIEI also trained a whole generation of indigenous intellectuals, many of whom are now influential leaders (for example, Luis Macas, the past president of CONAIE and the first indigenous member of the national Congress; José Quimbo, formerly a government indigenous representative; and Luis Monteluisa, the first national director of bilingual education). Many current local and community leaders also were trained during these adult literacy projects.

The adult literacy program backed by President Roldós may be considered one of the most important actions taken by an Ecuadoran government in support of indigenous people. Clearly, Roldós also benefited from the arrangement, as he won the support of the large indigenous sector in many areas. His administration coincided with the advent of the national indigenous organization. Other civil society organizations also benefited from the political space offered by his populist government. Roldós' administration created a generation of indigenous leadership, brought educated indigenous youth back to their communities, and facilitated the emergence of a new indigenous ideology in the country. The literacy program is discussed extensively in Chapter 5. Unfortunately, financial support for the program was cut after the death of President Roldós in a plane crash. "The adult education program was a positive experience," one leader stated, "but it was shot down with the death of the president."[24]

The Roldós administration created the first national Office of Indigenous Affairs in the Ministry of Social Welfare. Under previous administrations, indigenous issues were handled by the Campesino Office within the Ministry of Agriculture. The Office of Indigenous Affairs was meant to be the interlocutor between the administration and the indigenous organizations as well as a research center. The Office's creation signaled formal recognition of the importance of the indigenous rights issue; at the same time, it was a calculated political move to keep the support of the indigenous communities now that they were voters and their organized presence was growing.[25] The indigenous federations opposed the Office of Indigenous Affairs because they wanted direct access to government and resented having to go through the "paternalistic" office.[26]

Hurtado Administration

When Vice President Osvaldo Hurtado (1981-1984) became president after President Roldós died, relations between the indigenous communities and the government appear to have suffered. The center-left Hurtado, of the Popular Democracy Party (Democracia Popular — DP), was primarily concerned with making dramatic economic and political reforms in the time left to him. According to indigenous leaders, President Hurtado let their programs fall by the wayside: "After the death of Roldós, the program fell apart, that is, the guy who followed him either didn't care or didn't like it."[27] (The Office of Indigenous Affairs was not closed, but neither was it central to the Hurtado administration.) The fact that Hurtado could not run for re-election allowed him to push through many unpopular reforms that helped, he maintains, to consolidate democratic institutions. Hurtado remains an active intellectual and politician in Ecuador and in the region. He maintains a relationship with the U.S. Democratic Party through the Washington, D.C.-based Inter-American Dialogue. He defends his presidency, claiming that he continued to support the education and economic development of indigenous communities, as he did for all the subordinate classes. His discourse, however, clearly does not support special rights for indigenous people. In his analysis of the 1990 Uprising, for example, Hurtado states that the indigenous people's demands "go against the sovereign, unitary nature of the state as consecrated in the Constitution, and exclude the indigenous people from the economic and social processes that are essential for national development."[28]

Febres Cordero Administration

The conservative rightist and quite repressive (by Ecuadoran standards) government of León Febres Cordero (1984-1988) reversed many of the advances in government-indigenous relations. Agrarian reform was suspended, and land takeovers were repressed violently. Febres Cordero, of the National Reconstruction Front Party (Frente de Reconstrucción Nacional — FRN), supported some indigenous organizations that opposed ECUARUNARI, but his government is remembered for the repressive tactics he used against those who protested his harsh economic programs. Human rights organizations in Ecuador cite this period as one of increased arbitrary and illegal actions by government security forces. These violations included assassinations, torture, arbitrary arrests, and destruction of homes and property. Febres Cordero strengthened the national Office of Indigenous Affairs in an attempt to undermine the movement, and he created a parallel organization called Jatun Ayllu (Big Family). During his administration, a number of cases arose in which landowners' private guards tortured and assassinated indigenous community leaders and burned their homes. However, this administration's repression did not deter the indigenous people from organizing. CONAIE was consolidated during this period, and bilingual literacy work continued without state support. At the same time, international aid organizations began to support bilingual literacy projects and the indigenous organizations.

Borja Administration

Rodrigo Borja (1988-1992), like Roldós, came to power following a repressive regime and provided a democratic opening for the indigenous organizations. Although his administration was generally conciliatory toward the indigenous movement, it left enough promises and expectations unfulfilled to set the scene for the 1990 Uprising. Presdident Borja, of the Democratic Left Party (Izquierda Democrática — ID), replaced the Office of Indigenous Affairs with a Presidential Commission of Indigenous Affairs that was run by his nephew, Alfonso Calderón, who claimed to support the indigenous organizations and to have the complete trust of the president on this issue. The Borja government responded to the indigenous movement in three specific areas: education, territory, and legitimacy.[29]

In terms of legitimacy, the Borja administration immediately granted CONAIE recognition as the official representative of the indigenous people and began a series of dialogues with that organization. During 1988, indigenous and government representatives met almost every week. While the dialogues were inconsistent and in many ways unproductive, they provided a specific arena for direct debate between government officials and movement leaders. Indigenous delegates were received at the national palace, a powerful symbolic gesture considering that in much of rural Ecuador indigenous people usually were left unattended in government offices. However, such symbols of legitimacy did little to resolve specific problems such as land disputes, which had multiplied rapidly in the absence of repression and in response to an economic downturn. Even during the 1990 Uprising, President Borja exercised caution with the indigenous groups, controlling the army as much as possible to prevent violent repression, of which there was little, considering the magnitude of the upheaval. The government and CONAIE went back to the negotiating table, now with a higher profile and higher stakes.

The Borja administration also made important concessions to indigenous groups in terms of territory. The Ecuadoran Institute for Agrarian Reform and Colonization (Instituto Ecuatoriano de Reforma Agraria y Colonización — IERAC) had been "reactivated" to deal with land conflicts, but the process was still bogged down in bureaucracy, which led to numerous land disputes that eventually were brought to the negotiating table during the 1990 Uprising. In the Amazon, however, Borja was able to grant two extensive communal land concessions. The Huaorani people, among the most isolated nationalities, with only about 1,200 people, were given title to 600,000 hectares (about one-half of their traditional land). Later, after the OPIP march by the Quichua people of Pastaza province, mentioned earlier in this chapter, the government granted communal title to about 70 percent (1,115,475 hectares) of the territory the Quichua were demanding. While CONAIE leaders criticized the Borja government for bureaucratizing the land issue and for failing to take the dialogue seriously, Borja's administration, by taking some concrete steps in support of the indigenous movement, went beyond the actions of Roldós' administration.

Durán Ballén Administration

The economic liberalization policies implemented by President Sixto Durán Ballén (1992-1996) constituted a central platform of his administration. As in other countries, structural adjustment measures caused economic hardship, leading to increased political protest and crime and, I would argue, a generalized increase in violence. President Durán of the Social Christian Party (Partido Social Cristiano — PSC) followed the same neoliberal course within the context of his "modernization" plan; CONAIE adamantly protested his policies, claiming that the indigenous movement supported "modernization" of the government, but not "privatization."[30]

As analyst Adrián Bonilla warned, "If we do not understand the true dimension of violence in Ecuador . . . we run the risk of increased violence in society induced by the state."[31] Much of this violence was felt within the indigenous sector, as demonstrated by a rash of graffiti during Durán's administration, proclaiming the slogan, "Be a Patriot: Kill an Indian." Such graffiti suggested that the changing role of indigenous people in Ecuadoran society remained extremely controversial.

The government of Durán Ballén acknowledged the importance of the indigenous question in Ecuador but took direct steps to undermine the organizations. In his campaign, Durán (in contrast with Borja) rejected the concept of the pluri-national state. One of the first actions of his administration was an attempt to rescind the bilingual education accord with CONAIE, but mass protests changed that policy to one of restructuring.

Durán did open an office to administer his policies in the indigenous communities, and this division became the Special Office for Indigenous Affairs for the president. Furthermore, Durán named an indigenous intellectual, José Quimbo, as its director. Quimbo maintained a direct line to President Durán through his daughter, Alicia Durán, who often traveled with Quimbo to indigenous communities. The Special Office for Indigenous Affairs had few economic resources, limiting Quimbo's ability to respond to indigenous people's requests, and few indigenous communities had any contact with this office.[32] CONAIE leaders denounced the office as a way to undermine their organization, claiming that Quimbo did not represent them and arguing that they should be allowed to choose their own representative.

Meanwhile, the IERAC remained unresponsive to land conflicts during Durán's administration, and violence escalated. The case of Yuracruz is an unfortunate example. The IERAC had ruled in favor of granting a land title to the Yuracruz indigenous association years before but still had not come up with the required financial backing when the landowners hired "security guards" in November 1992.

The security guards of the Parachute Security Company burned houses, stole animals, and tortured members of the indigenous association; these conflicts resulted in the deaths of 14 Yuracruz people. Almost all of the association members were forced to abandon the land. No government intervention took place until human rights organizations made an international denunciation of rapes committed by the guards, including rapes of two elderly women (77 and 91 years old) that led to their deaths.[33] Durán, in fact, had agreed to provide the financial help necessary to resolve the problem during a dialogue with CONAIE in December 1992, but no resolution occurred until after the deaths of the two women.

The Durán administration differed from the Borja government in its response to indigenous mobilization. As mentioned above, Borja received CONAIE leaders in the national palace as legal representatives of the indigenous population. In contrast, under Durán, when CONAIE and FENOC led a march to Congress on June 9, 1993, to present their alternative agrarian reform proposal, the marchers were met with tear gas and beatings and were denied entrance. Quimbo's office made no attempt to intervene and made no public comment on this or any of the many other cases of repression of indigenous communities, thus bringing the office's political autonomy into question.

The Armed Forces

The armed forces, it should be noted, have their own relationship with the indigenous sector, separate from the government's relationship. Since the 1990 Uprising, military presence in the indigenous communities has increased, and the military has officially begun a campaign of "civic action" that resembles the civic action programs taught to foreign militaries at the U.S. Army School of the Americas. This project has involved the military in development projects in the community, and the armed forces have entered into agreements with cabildos and, in some cases, with the federations themselves.

In the Amazon, the military often serves as an arbiter in land conflicts and between oil companies and indigenous federations. In many parts of the country, the military has provided logistical support, such as rice and tents, for large assemblies. At the same time, the overall policy of the military toward indigenous people supports assimilation. Reflecting that view, Durán's Minister of Defense José Gallardo, compared problems with indigenous people in Ecuador to ethnic conflicts in Europe and offered the following suggestion for Ecuador:

"Look at how different nationalities are confronting each other and fighting in the old Europe. What we need to do is melt together all of the different races that come to our country with the natives to create one complex human type."[34]

Despite the relative autonomy of the armed forces in Ecuador, the government does have some influence over levels of repression. While Borja was able to keep repression at an impressively low level during the 1990 Uprising, Durán did not demonstrate the same level of commitment to avoiding violence.

Military repression against indigenous people in Ecuador is not comparable to the level of violence in most countries where indigenous people have become important political actors, including Guatemala, Mexico, and Colombia. This can be attributed to the unusually populist/nationalist military culture in Ecuador that was inherited by General Velasco Ibarra. The military often states its position: that the military's job is to defend the Ecuadoran people, not the government. Of course, the position of each administration is influential, as indicated by the difference between the Borja and the Durán administrations. However, the Ecuadoran military does retain significant autonomy from civilian control.[35]

INDIGENOUS PEOPLE AND THE ELECTORAL PROCESS

Indigenous leaders are engaged in an ongoing debate about participation in political parties. A number of parties, particularly on the left, have promoted indigenous candidates in local elections and have forged alliances with indigenous communities. The Broad Leftist Front (Frente Amplio de la Izquierda — FADI) and the Popular Democratic Movement Party (Movimiento Popular Democrático — MPD) have been particularly active in promoting ties. The indigenous federations have maintained a general policy of not sponsoring candidates. They argue that party interests may go against those of the federations, and experience has demonstrated that as a minority within the system, they can do little to make changes. Indigenous federations generally agree that, in the final analysis, political parties do not represent indigenous interests. As indigenous leader Luis Maldonado said, referring to the 1992 election, "When our brothers were assassinated, the political parties in the National Congress, including those on the left, did not speak up or take action in the name of justice."[36] CONAIE explains that it cannot affiliate with a party because it represents indigenous people at the national level.

In 1996, indigenous groups surprised many onlookers by forming a new political movement to participate in electoral politics — the Pachakutik Movement for Pluri-national Unity.[37] Although the movement is not registered as a political party, it functions essentially as an electoral coalition of indigenous and other social movement groups. Not only did the movement participate in the 1996 national elections, but Luis Macas, CONAIE leader and outspoken critic of indigenous participation in elections, ran as the Pachakutik candidate for national deputy (member of Congress) and won. Why this sudden shift?

In reality, the shift was not so sudden; rather, it resulted from a combination of external and internal factors. Internally, Ecuador's indigenous leaders sensed their growing political power and were increasingly anxious to express it. Externally, Bolivia had elected a member of the Aymara indigenous group, Víctor Hugo Cárdenas, as vice president in 1993.[38] His position inspired the continental indigenous movement to reconsider participation in electoral politics. In December 1993, the IV National CONAIE Congress was held at the CONFENIAE headquarters near Puyo in the Amazon. Amazonian leaders tended to be vociferous about the need to launch indigenous candidates, and they used their majority presence at the Puyo Congress to push the point. Cárdenas had planned to attend, but at the last minute he sent his wife, Lidia Catari de Cárdenas, an imposing Aymaran leader in her own right. She told stories about how she shocked her colleagues at the national palace in La Paz by insisting on wearing her traditional dress. She encouraged the Congress participants to consider seriously participating in the elections, exhorting them: "The time to be ruled is over. It is now time to rule."[39] The debate about electoral participation was pushed to the top of the agenda, although no final decision was made until the CONAIE Congress in Cotopaxi three years later. In the March 1996 national elections, CONAIE's Macas won his seat in Congress along with seven other candidates, both indigenous and nonindigenous, from the Pachakutik/Nuevo País coalition. Seats were won by Pachakutik throughout the country in all but one province.

Pachakutik representatives were elected at all other levels of government throughout the country, both in 1996 and again in 1998. Pachakutik also won seven seats on the 1998 Constitutional Assembly, where they were vociferous contributors to changes in the national Constitution.

Indigenous representatives in Ecuador have wielded a surprising amount of influence despite having fewer than 10 representatives in the 123-member Congress. This is due, in part, to the weak political system, regional

CONAIE spreads a new indigenous ideology.

divisions, and fighting among parties, as Jennifer Collins has pointed out.[40] The indigenous influence in Congress is also due to the powerful social movement that, in general, backs the indigenous representatives. The Pachakutik representatives, who call themselves the "indigenous block" in Congress, try to meet weekly with the leadership of CONAIE to coordinate political strategies. The coordination has led to, among other things, the adaptation of the national Constitution to recognize Ecuador as a pluri-national state.

An increasing number of difficulties are also associated with partici-pation in the electoral process. Many of the veteran leaders were nominated for political positions, leaving some indigenous organizations without experienced leadership. Disagreements have emerged between the indig-enous representatives, who are anxious to take advantage of their newly acquired political positions, and their organizations' blanket statements about corruption in the Ecuadoran political apparatus. In the January 2000 Uprising, for example, the indigenous social movements were calling for a complete dissolution of Congress, a call that the Pachakutik representatives had trouble agreeing with.

Future observations will shed light on the utility of electoral participa-tion for obtaining indigenous rights in Ecuadoran society. The questions remain: Is indigenous participation in an unstable system, in fact, strength-ening or weakening the indigenous movement, and is indigenous participa-tion strengthening or weakening civil society in general?

Although the impact of indigenous participation in electoral politics is outside the scope of this book, it provides an exciting opportunity for further study.

Conclusions

The relations between indigenous people and the state in Ecuador have developed within a framework of differing concepts of citizenship and nationality. The state has a project of establishing political and social hegemony for the Hispanic Ecuadoran elite.[41] Since Ecuador's indepen-dence, the political elite has had the project of creating a national identity and a set of institutions to support it. The democratic institutions of the state are still weak, particularly outside the urban areas.

Moreover, the state remains highly centralized, with little control or financial resources in the countryside. According to the indigenous federa-tions, the construction of a national identity is also weak in the indigenous communities where, CONAIE argues, inhabitants derive little benefit from being Ecuadoran citizens. Electoral abstention among the indigenous popu-lation is high. In 1984, for example, abstention in the indigenous populated areas averaged 50 percent, as compared to the national average of 21 percent.[42]

In the context of a weak state, lacking strong institutions and having to count on limited loyalty outside the cities, it appears that Ecuadoran government officials feel threatened by many proposals made by the indigenous movement. For example, the concept of a pluri-national state, one of CONAIE's central ideological proposals, does not seem so radical when one considers that such states exist in various forms throughout the world, and they include some of the most democratic and stable countries, such as Canada, Switzerland, and the United States. Many Native American tribes in the United States have some degree of sovereignty. But given the relative weakness of the Ecuadoran state and the global context of disintegrating nations (for example, the former Yugoslavia and the former Soviet Union), the Ecuadoran government has had trouble accepting the pluri-national proposal. The concepts of autonomy and self-determination for indigenous people are perceived by many Ecuadorans as threatening to the integrity of the "nation."

The general official response, even from fairly sympathetic presidents such as Roldós and Borja, is to integrate indigenous issues into the government and to prevent the establishment of authorities outside government institutions. This has taken place at the national level as well as at the provincial level, where a number of local governments have opened offices of indigenous affairs. Some indigenous leaders see this as a way to co-opt a movement that is attempting to provide alternatives to the present system of government. For others, this is a legitimate way to gain political space for indigenous people within the existing state.

The indigenous movement separated from the political left because the left did not support cultural differences; the movement then made cultural demands on the government. The government was prepared to confront armed subversion, but it did not consider that organizing based on culture might lead to political power. By now, "cultural resistance" has created the most important social movement in Ecuador. Through bilingual education and countless demonstrations of political sophistication, the indigenous movement has reinvented what it means to be "Indian." Now it remains for the government to integrate the proposals of the indigenous movement and for the movement to maintain the political space it has won.

Notes

1. The United Federation of Workers represents the three largest trade union federations and is the most important workers' organization in Ecuador.

2. Juan Pablo Moncagatta, 1993, op-ed article, *Hoy*, June 2.

3. *Weapons of the Weak* by James Scott (1985, New Haven, Conn.: Yale University Press) contains one of the most important discussions of what Scott calls "everyday forms of resistance."

4. Andrés Guerrero, 1993, "La desintigración de la administración étnica en el Ecuador," in *Sismo étnico en el Ecuador: Varias perspectivas*, ed. CEDIME (Centro de Investigaciones de los Movimientos Sociales del Ecuador) (Quito: Abya-Yala), 7-28.

5. See Héctor Díaz-Polanco, 1987, "*Neoindigenismo* and the Ethnic Question in Central America," *Latin American Perspectives* 14 (1), for an interesting discussion of the independent indigenous perspective, particularly the role of what he considers to be the deleterious impact of some U.S. indigenous involvements in Central America. Ward Churchill is an important indigenous intellectual representative of what Díaz-Polanco calls the "Fourth World" independent indigenous perspective.

6. Humberto Muenala, 1993, Bilingual Intercultural Education Project, interview by author.

7. For more on new social movements in Latin America, see S. E. Álvarez, E. Dagnino, and A. Escobar, 1998, *Cultures of Politics, Politics of Cultures: Revisioning Latin America's Social Movements* (Boulder, Colo.: Westview Press). The relationship between class and ethnicity in terms of the indigenous movement is developed further in Chapters 4 and 5 of this book..

8. Anthony Bebbington, et al., 1992, "De la protesta a la productividad: Evolución de las federaciones indígenas del Ecuador," *Desarrollo de Base* 16 (2): 11-21.

9. CONAIE (Confederation of Indigenous Nationalities of Ecuador), 1989, *Las nacionalidades indígenas en el Ecuador: Nuestro proceso organizativo* (Quito: Abya-Yala), 213-234.

10. Galo Ramón Valarezo, 1992, "Estado plurinacional: Una propuesta innovadora atrapada en viejos conceptos," in *Pueblos Indios, Estado y Derecho*, ed. Corporación Editora Nacional (Quito: Abya-Yala), 9.

11. CONAIE 1989, 260.

12. León Zamosc, 1994, "Estadística de las áreas de predominio étnico de la Sierra Ecuatoriana," Sociology Department, University of California, San Diego, unpublished paper, 301.

13. Oxfam America provides privately raised funds and technical help to local organizations around the world dedicated to helping poor people move out of poverty. See <http://www.oxfamamerica.org/about/index.html.>

14. The Uprising of June 1990 will be shortened throughout to the 1990 Uprising.

15. See, for instance, CEDIME, 1993, *Sismo étnico en el Ecuador: Varias perspectivas* (Quito: Abya-Yala); Segundo Moreno Yánez and José Figueroa, 1992, *El Levantamiento Indígena del Inti-Raymi* (Quito: Abya-Yala); Diego Cornejo, 1991, *INDIOS: Una reflexión sobre el Levantamiento Indígena de 1990* (Quito: Logos); and Diego Cornejo, 1993, *Los indios y el Estado-País: Pluriculturalidad y multietnicidad en el Ecuador: Contribuciones al debate* (Quito: Abya-Yala).

16. José Almeida, 1993, "El Levantamiento Indígena como momento constituvo nacional," in *Sismo étnico en el Ecuador: Varias perspectivas*, ed. CEDIME (Quito: Abya-Yala), 8.

17. Agricultural engineer Rubén Espinosa Román speaking to the Dairy Association of the Sierra (this association is one of the most outspoken opponents of CONAIE), as reported in *El Comercio*, June 28, 1990.

18. Luis Monteluisa, 1993, director, Direction of Bilingual Intercultural Education, interview by author.

19. The political impact of bilingual education is discussed thoroughly in Chapter 5.

20. Almeida 1993, 10.

21. Juan Arévalo, 1993, Bolívar Campesino Federation, interview by author.

22. Zamosc 1993, 283.

23. Luis Macas, 1993, president of CONAIE, interview by author; and Alberto Andrango, 1991, National Federation of Campesino and Indigenous Organizations (FENOC-I), interview by author.

24. Héctor Villamil, 1993, Organization of Indigenous Peoples of Pastaza (OPIP), interview by author.

25. Alicia Ibarra, 1991, sociologist working in the office of President Jaime Roldós, interview by author.

26. Fabián Muenala, 1991, Indigenous intellectual at CONAIE, interview by author.

27. Macas, 1993, interview by author.

28. *El Universo*, 1991, March 4.

29. This section relies on 1991 interviews conducted by the author with Borja administration officials Gonzalo Ortiz, minister of government; Leonardo Calderón; Luis Luna Gaybor, Ecuadoran Institute of Agrarian Reform and Colonization; and Alfonso Calderón, architect.

30. Melecio Santos, 1991, vice-president of CONAIE, interview by author.

31. Adrián Bonilla, 1993, "Internal Security and Society: Are We in Danger?" *Hoy* April 25.

32. Based on the author's field research.

33. *CONAIE Bulletin*, March 9, 1993.

34. *Hoy*, 1993, June 24.

35. In January 2000, President Mahuad was ousted by a unique indigenous/military alliance. That mobilization is beyond the scope of this study, but it is important to note that relationships had developed between indigenous and military leadership. The alliance was formed with midlevel military command, and it was disbanded quickly by the highest military commander.

36. Luis Maldonado, 1993, "Indígenas y elecciones 1992," in *Sismo étnico en el Ecuador: Varias perspectivas*, ed. CEDIME (Quito: Abya Yala), 306.

37. As to the spelling of Pachakutik, since Quichua was not a written language, linguists continue to debate the spelling of Quichua words; thus there are inconsistencies. Readers may find transliterations of Quichua words spelled differently, for example, "Pachacutic" or "Kichua."

38. Bolivian President Gonzalo Sánchez de Lozada's running mate in the June 1993 election was Víctor Hugo Cárdenas, Ayamaran leader of the Túpaj Katarí Revolutionary Liberation Movement (Movimiento Revolucionario Túpaj Katarí de Liberación — MRTKL).

39. Author's field notes.

40. Jennifer Collins, 2000, "A Sense of Possibility: Ecuador's Indigenous Movement Takes Center Stage," *NACLA Report on the Americas*, Vol. XXXIII, No. 5, March/April, 40-46.

41. See Mary Crain, 1990, "The Social Construction of National Identity in Highland Ecuador," *Anthropological Quarterly* 63 (1): 43-59, for an interesting analysis of Ecuador in a Gramscian/anthropological framework.

42. Erwin Frank, Nina Patiño, and Marta Rodríguez, 1992, *Los políticos y los indígenas* (Quito: Abya-Yala/ILDIS — Instituto Latinoamericano de Investigaciones Sociales).

Chapter 4

The 1990 Indigenous Uprising in Ecuador: Politicized Ethnicity as Social Movement

INTRODUCTION

The indigenous movement in Ecuador developed in a context of exclusion that was exacerbated by contradictions in the government projects of nation building and construction of pluralist democracy. Starting from that context, the indigenous people of Ecuador have developed a contemporary identity, based on an ideology that recognizes their rights as a distinct people and also as citizens. This chapter will examine how those factors established the conditions for mobilization of indigenous people in Ecuador in a dramatic political moment for their movement: the 1990 Uprising. Although other indigenous mass protests have occurred since 1990, this historic event set the stage for the future leadership of CONAIE.

During the summer of 1990, indigenous communities took center stage in Ecuadoran politics with a week-long uprising that virtually closed transportation along the main roads in the Highlands region. This 1990 Uprising demonstrated that the indigenous people had created a political space for themselves in a nation-state regime that excluded them from any significant political participation. Like other modern social movements in Latin America, indigenous communities succeeded in organizing, based on a common collective identity to reach political objectives.

Despite economic and political crises, organized resistance and collective action throughout Latin America have encountered a wide variety of responses. In the last few decades, strategies for popular resistance have taken many forms, from self-help organizations to demands for participation independent of political parties (as civil society representatives) in constitutional assemblies. The growing range of types of political protest has caused analysts to reconsider the traditional concepts regarding social movements, which were based on struggles for formal political power in structures that could be changed only through large social upheavals such as revolutions.[1] Analytical discussions of social movements should consider the complexities of relationships between societal and governmental actors, and the formation of collective identities in the political sphere. This chapter analyzes the 1990 Uprising in the context of such discussions. The events and the ideas of the participants in the 1990 Uprising are considered here to be aspects of a larger societal process that surfaced and became more observable during the political moment under discussion. The objective is not only to explain the 1990 Uprising, but also to use it in considering how ethnicity can become a mobilizing agent for a social movement.

In the case of Ecuador, and in other indigenous mobilizations throughout the continent, ethnic identity has emerged as a salient issue for political mobilization. When we consider ethnic identity to be fluid, then the mobilization of ethnic identity in a political struggle can be considered a type of resource mobilization by a "new social movement." These two general paradigms — new social movements and resource mobilization theory — often are interpreted as contradictory perspectives, as in Jean Cohen's instructive essay that differentiates social movement theorists who focus on *strategies* from those who focus on *identity*.[2] The following examination of the 1990 Uprising will demonstrate that, in fact, the two perspectives can be complementary, particularly in explaining the phenomenon of ethnic politics. The indigenous movement, although based on formation of a collective identity, is constrained by real resource variables. Likewise, by pursuing strategic political actions, the movement contributes to changing social constructs of identity.

Social science literature concerning social movements often is dichotomized between structuralist positions in the Marxist tradition or idea-driven positions in the Weberian tradition. This dichotomy between materialism-driven or idea-driven collective action can be found at the root of current debates contrasting European-based concepts of new social movements and U.S.-based theories of collective action, in particular that of "resource mobilization." However, this dichotomy is too simplistic to resonate within real situations. Analysis of any specific case reveals that both materialist and ideological factors are relevant to social movements; the interplay between material and ideological factors defines the political sphere, to rephrase a paradigm proposed by Antonio Gramsci.[3] Likewise, as this chapter will demonstrate, ethnicity is both an ideology in terms of collective identity and a structural variable in terms of resources.

The indigenous movement in Ecuador strives to create alliances for collective action based on identity, rather than seek what traditionally has been conceived of as class-based alliances. While class alliances are still relevant, particularly in forming alliances with other sectors of society to achieve broader goals, the general trend of the movement has been from campesino to indigenous in orientation.[4] This study's analysis will support the theory that ethnic identity is a *fluid* or *situational* concept, particularly in a political context.

Theories attempting to describe ethnic politics too often have focused on a static perception of ethnicity. By considering ethnicity as a structural variable, these theories exclude the useful framework of competing or transforming identities. When ethnicity is understood as a constructed identity, the complexities of identity politics as an ideological struggle can be highlighted. Ethnic identity, it will be demonstrated, is itself a potential political resource. The situational aspect of ethnic identity can be clarified to some degree by causal explanations, such as resource mobilization theory. However, it must also be understood as an ideological variable that is influenced, but not constrained, by structural variables.

The fluid nature of ethnicity, as it is used for political mobilization, is an important factor for understanding the 1990 Indigenous Uprising. Another factor to be considered here is government policy toward the indigenous movement. Too much theoretical literature about Latin American politics focuses on politics from "above" or "below" without enough attention to the relationship between the two. Politics must be understood as a relationship between social pressures and government activity. This relationship functions within a complicated societal context that could be described in terms of political culture. However, this analysis will focus on interactions between indigenous and government actors, and, to some extent, on the way they influence societal concepts of what is "indigenous."

The relationship between the government and civil society is key to the analysis of the 1990 Uprising. This chapter focuses on the social movement, with less attention to the political regimes, described in Chapter 3. However, social movements function not in a vacuum, but in constant relation to political systems. Government is a contributing factor in the political mobilization of indigenous people. Likewise, as with other social movements, the political struggles of indigenous communities are reshaping what is conceived of as political space, and societal conceptions of social groups are being reshaped in the process.[5]

The following discussion of the 1990 Uprising will highlight various factors in the relationship between the government and indigenous people that have influenced the movement. I contend that through participation in the movement, indigenous communities have contributed to the redefinition of their own collective identity and have reshaped the way they are perceived by Ecuadoran society. Organization of a collective political movement based on ethnic identity has provided a means for indigenous people to achieve political representation and access to material benefits.

THE 1990 UPRISING

The success of the 1990 Indigenous Uprising that shook Ecuador in the summer of 1990 surprised even its organizers and has proved to be a turning point in the political process of the indigenous communities. This Uprising was surprising not only in terms of its magnitude, but also in terms of its wholly indigenous nature; that is, it grew out of a movement clearly defined along ethnic lines. How is it that Ecuador has such a clearly defined ethnic movement, when its neighbors, even those with high-density indigenous populations (such as Bolivia, Peru, and Guatemala), tend to have organizations based on class or other issues? Why did the 1990 Uprising happen when it did, and what were the consequences? How has government policy contributed to the shaping of the indigenous movement, and vice versa? These questions will be answered in this chapter.

The 1990 Indigenous Uprising officially took place from June 4 through June 6, 1990, although it actually extended for a few weeks before and after those dates. It began with the occupation of Santo Domingo Cathedral in Quito, during which a list of demands (see Appendix 4) was presented to the government by indigenous organizations. Although the cathedral's occupation and 10-day hunger strike resulted from a local initiative from Chimborazo and originally was not conceived by CONAIE as a part of the 1990 Uprising, it served as a catalyst for the mobilizations that spread throughout the country, especially in the Sierra.

CONAIE had quietly spread the word to its affiliates, as a result of a decision made at the April 1990 national CONAIE Assembly, urging all indigenous communities to participate in whatever manner they could in a forthcoming national Uprising. The main motive was to demand that the government address the many land conflicts that the agrarian reform institute (IERAC) had not resolved in a timely manner. CONAIE also made a series of other, more general and ideological demands, and provincial organizations presented specific demands addressing local problems to their local governments.

Communities responded with roadblocks, boycotts of markets, occupations of local government offices, land invasions (called *recuperation of land* by the indigenous groups, as from their perspective these lands were theirs in the first place), marches, and even the kidnapping of military personnel. Because the national organization had not called for a specific type of participation in the Uprising, substantial local initiatives took place. The decentralized character of the 1990 Uprising allowed for the influence of historical and traditional forms of protest, as well as forms of protest specific to the needs of different communities. This decentralization proved to be instrumental in the success of the various communities' actions and to the success of the Uprising viewed in its entirety.

In the province of Bolívar, for example, protesters cut the water pipes to the provincial capital, leaving the city without water for three days. In the province of Chimborazo, 30 militiamen were detained and forced to walk barefoot to a hiding place where they were kept, unharmed, as leverage to ensure the release of indigenous activists taken as prisoners by the government. In some cases in which protesters were arrested, indigenous people stormed police stations, demanding their release. In Cotapaxi, shell horns, a traditional means of convocation, were used to guide people from villages to the gathering place for the march.[6]

Despite the vast variety of forms of resistance demonstrated by the participants in the 1990 Uprising, success was measured, for the most part, by more standard indicators, namely, the great number of indigenous people involved and the response of the government. Along with the thousands that gathered at the marches (an estimated 50,000 in Riobamba and smaller, but equally impressive numbers elsewhere), there were enough committed people to carry out the often-dangerous direct political actions. Land invasions, for example, were numerous, demonstrating the agrarian-conflict roots of the indigenous movement. Forty land takeovers were realized in the provinces of Pichincha and Imbabura alone.[7] After about a week of protests, the national indigenous organization and the government agreed to a dialogue, and the Uprising was officially called off. This response by the government, and the fact that the president himself agreed to sit down at the negotiating table with CONAIE, represented to the public the success of the 1990 Uprising and the powerful political space the organization had won.

Throughout the Highlands, indigenous communities rose up in non-violent resistance, but what exactly were they resisting? Ecuador does not appear to suffer from the endemic violence that some of its neighbors endure. Although it suffers from the underdevelopment and unequal distribution of wealth common to developing countries, it has the benefit of an oil reserve that keeps the economy afloat. The social democratic government of President Rodrigo Borja was not overtly repressive, and, in fact, his administration took significant steps toward integrating the issues of the indigenous population into the government's structure. It is my contention that structural, political, and cultural influences account for the success of the 1990 Uprising, and these influences were expressed through politicized ethnicity. The structural issues to which the 1990 Uprising responded vary from community to community, but the growing consciousness of a common identity and thus a common struggle is what made the 1990 Uprising a national movement.

The indigenous organizations involved cited ideological causes for the 1990 Uprising, such as discrimination. Still, clear, structural underlying causes for the mobilization formed the bases for those general causes related to discrimination. As with most indigenous struggles, the central issue was *land*. Although it must be kept in mind that land is a base that is as much cultural as economic for indigenous peoples, in this study, "land" is referred to primarily in the context of an economic base. Throughout Ecuador's history, the effects of colonization, land oligarchy, and ineffective agrarian reform have led indigenous communities to engage in long struggles for more land.

One causal theory for the 1990 unrest, often cited by analysts, refers to the economic recession Ecuador was suffering. According to this perspective, many indigenous people who left to seek employment in urban areas had returned to the countryside, thus stimulating increased unrest over the shortage of land for peasants. However, while demographic pressure in the countryside clearly was a contributing factor to the many land conflicts, such pressure came not from the recession so much as from the historic unequal distribution of land.[8] Also, inflation caused the rapid devaluation of agricultural products produced by indigenous communities, which contributed to the tension. Clearly, as well, the scarcity of fundamental human material necessities — for infrastructure, water, and education — played an important role in the mobilizationand headed the list of needs in most indigenous communities.

The above complaints, however, which can be called the *structural* causes, were not the only or even the most common answers given to my interview questions concerning reasons for participation in the 1990 Uprising. More common were answers such as these: "We want to be treated with respect"; "for dignity"; "we demand equality"; "we deserve the same attention that mestizos are given by the government"; or simply, "so they will begin to listen to us." Answers like these, because they address identity and culture, demonstrate that the movement was concerned with what I call *ideological* issues and not only with structural issues such as the economic crisis. Poverty is a structural condition throughout rural Ecuador; however, clearly, the 1990 Uprising was not solely about poverty.

In the southern province of Loja, for example, land conflicts are not as salient an issue as in other regions, yet participation in the 1990 Uprising there was notably high. According to witnesses I interviewed, some members of the minority nonindigenous (mestizo) community felt so threatened by the 1990 Uprising that they attacked indigenous protesters with guns. Luckily, the indigenous people saw them coming and were able to hide out in the trees. When the mestizos ran out of ammunition, the indigenous protesters chased them back into the town, throwing rocks. "They felt terrorized," explained a local indigenous leader. "We didn't attack them directly, but they were so sure we were going to kick all the mestizos out of town that some of them had packed suitcases waiting by the door!"[9] It is notable that in this instance, where structural issues such as land access were probably least relevant to the Uprising, one of the most intense episodes of interethnic violence erupted.

It should be noted that the armed confrontation in Loja province was an exception; the 1990 Uprising was nonviolent on the whole. In most areas, the protesters even received some support from nonindigenous sectors of the population. In some cases, this support came in the form of food or supplies. In Quito and Guayaquil, students and workers joined in the marches. In all the provinces, though, tension between the indigenous and mestizo populations was notable during the Uprising; the tension was usually explained, in interviews with members of both populations, as "a lack of understanding."

Loja provides an example in which racial discrimination became a causal factor in the 1990 Uprising. In that case, the two ethnic groups actually confronted each other in a dramatization of daily ethnic conflict. Many participants gave examples of existing discrimination against indigenous people: They were forced to sit in the back of buses, they were not received in government offices, they were ridiculed for their language or clothing, they were not given fair prices at the market, and so on. Much of the anger expressed in the Uprising was in response to this discrimination.

Evidence from the interviews conducted suggests that although the 1990 Uprising was a response to various structural concerns in different regions, the ideological cause (in this case indigenous identity) made the Uprising a national movement that went beyond local concerns. Luis Macas, who served as president of CONAIE at that time, explained, "We consider the economic problems . . . are tools for the struggle that allow us to go beyond the resolution of immediate problems to allow us to advance further along with our political proposals."[10] As Jorge León has pointed out, the 1990 Uprising had a "multiplicity of meanings for the actors,"[11] according to their different circumstances, but it became a national movement based on *identity*. Clearly, the conflict was both structural and ideological in nature. While discrimination obviously is not new to Ecuador, political mobilization based on identity brought the issue to the forefront of national politics.

CAUSAL FACTORS: FROM "ABOVE" AND "BELOW"

The 1990 Uprising established a political space for indigenous actors on the national political agenda. The demand for this type of space can be understood, according to Elizabeth Jelin, as "a struggle to widen sociopolitical citizenship."[12] In most cases, this means guaranteeing a voice for the people represented, in a government from which they otherwise feel excluded. According to democratic standards, the majority of indigenous people do not have the rights of citizenship in Ecuador. Only in 1979 were they given the opportunity to vote for the first time. As one young indigenous leader remarked, "We have no rights here; we live like Palestinians."[13] At the same time, indigenous people arguably represent the most organized social sector in Ecuadoran society; therefore, considered collectively, they may be considered a sound example of civil society in relation to the state.

In the analysis of causal explanations of a social movement, it is important to study how civil society and the state influence each other. The interaction between the state and civil society actually is a struggle over terms of the broader form of citizenship for which the social movement strives. The struggle takes place in structural and ideological arenas. In this case, it concerns a reconceptualization of indigenous people in national society. The 1990 Uprising was a political manifestation of this battle.

Political explanations for the 1990 Uprising come both from the government (above), and from the indigenous movement (below). The growing capacity of the indigenous movement has not been isolated from changes in state policies. In turn, the government has been influenced by the movement. Regarding the government, three influential factors should be noted: unrealized expectations, the contradictions of nation building, and underestimation of culture as a political variable. The last two factors were analyzed in a general way in Chapters 2 and 3; now they can be applied to assist our understanding of the 1990 Uprising.

Unrealized Expectations

Considering the ineffectiveness of government policy, the factor of unrealized expectations must be cited as a specific cause of the 1990 Uprising. A number of steps taken early on by the Borja administration encouraged the indigenous communities to believe that their situation would improve. Clearly, at the least, Borja meant to give the impression that he would improve the situation of the indigenous population. As Macas of CONAIE commented afterward: "Dr. Rodrigo Borja and his people had created a series of expectations for our people and for us as well. We said, with this government we are going to be in the thousand miracles, and we made proposals like you can't imagine, voluminous folders, so that our demands could be attended to. . . ."[14]

Soon, however, it became evident to indigenous leaders that the Borja administration was not going to be able to follow through on all of its intentions. Three clear examples are provided by the policies on political dialogue, bilingual education, and land reform policy.

Within a few days of assuming office, on August 10, 1988, Borja set up a Presidential Commission of Indigenous Affairs, directed by his nephew, Alfonso Calderón. The main function of the commission was to establish and maintain direct contact with indigenous groups.[15] CONAIE was recognized officially as the legal representative of the indigenous people, which gave the organization legitimacy as a political actor in Ecuadoran society. Thereafter, a regular dialogue procedure was set up to negotiate relations between the indigenous sectors and the government. The dialogues took the form of weekly meetings between CONAIE and three presidential aides who were experienced in indigenous affairs, but who did not hold high-level positions in the government. Although important agreements were made, particularly concerning bilingual education, the dialogue began to break down after about one year. CONAIE representatives complained that the presidential commission was ineffective and did not hold enough decision-making power. The commission, they asserted, was concerned only with segmented issues such as education, but not with the principal issues, mainly that of the pluri-national character of the state. The president, according to CONAIE leaders, was unwilling to meet directly with them.[16] The commission, in turn, complained that CONAIE was making unreasonable demands. By the time of the 1990 Uprising, the commission had not met with CONAIE for more than six months.[17]

Another example of unmet expectations aroused by the Borja government was the area of bilingual education. One of the most celebrated results of the dialogue was the formation of the National Directorate of Bilingual Intercultural Education (Dirección Nacional de Educación Intercultural Bilingüe — DINEIB), directed by CONAIE. The directorate institutionalized bilingual education programs, which had been going on in experimental form throughout the country, and proposed the participation of indigenous educators in the development of the program. An agreement was signed, allocating 800 million sucres (about $800,000) to bilingual, bicultural education for 1989 and 2,800 million sucres for 1990, thus demonstrating the government's commitment to that process.

The total amount of allocated resources never arrived, however, according to CONAIE leaders. The directorate became a huge bureaucracy that served to dissipate the political strength of the bilingual education process. Indigenous organizations had to fight to maintain their influence over bilingual education, as mentioned previously.[18] The directorate served an important political function, and bilingual education changed the nature of local politics in rural Ecuador. At the same time, the directorate's administration was weak, not only due to lack of funds, but also because of the political nature of what should have been a technical administrative office. As a result, indigenous communities expressed frustration with the bilingual education system.

The large number of unresolved land conflicts also produced frustrations. According to IERAC, the Borja administration had resolved 1.5

million hectares of land disputes, with 1.2 million of those in favor of indigenous communities. The main land reform problem addressed by indigenous organizations is that although land might be legally adjudicated to indigenous communities, little or nothing is done to protect that adjudication, and communities still find themselves fighting and dying for land that is legally theirs. Early in the Borja administration, an impressive communal land title (the largest in the history of Ecuador, according to the director of the Agrarian Reform Institute, Luis Luna)[19] was given to an indigenous group in the Amazon, the Huaorani. The land title, while generally applauded, still denied the indigenous people any control over exploitation of natural resources or development, and oil companies have constructed a highly disputed road through the Huaorani territory. That new land title also failed to respond to problems of colonization produced by the 1973 Agrarian Reform Law. The government continued to divide the Amazon, including indigenous areas, into development-oriented zones.[20] It seemed apparent that even though the administration was taking some legal steps in favor of the indigenous people, for most communities nothing had changed for the better. The resulting disillusionment was one of the principal factors contributing to the 1990 Uprising.

Simplifying things somewhat, this is a case of relative deprivation as a causal factor. Ted Gurr underlies the importance of the actors' *perceptions* of "the discrepancy between their value expectations and their value capabilities."[21] The indigenous communities responded to the failed expectation for increased political attention as well as to the lack of improvement in their material conditions. While this is a useful framework in which to view the breakdown in dialogue, relative deprivation does not, however, explain the complexities of the situation. The relative deprivation explanation gives only limited insight because it fails to explain the dynamics of the movement and the ideological factors that influenced it.

Contradictions of Nation Building

A second important factor contributing to the context that set the stage for the 1990 Uprising is linked to the model of nation building that still persists in Ecuador. The Ecuadoran state finds itself in a paradox common to other developing countries. On the one hand, it is pursuing democratic reforms based on models of pluralism and participation, just the types of goals that have motivated Latin American new social movements.[22] At the same time, the state is continuing a process of nation building that calls for the development of a national citizenry and the establishment of political hegemony.

A concise example of this paradox was provided by a discussion with Luis Luna Gaybor, the director of IERAC.[23] He proudly explained that his institute had given more communal land to indigenous communities than had any previous administration. A few minutes later, discussing the pluri-national character of Ecuador, he assured me that it was temporary and that within a few generations the remaining indigenous people would "disap-pear"; that is, they would be integrated successfully into the nation. The pluralist-democracy model led him to respond to the specific needs of indigenous people with communal land grants, but, at the same time, the nation-building model urged cultural integration.[24] The contemporary in-digenous movement emerged, in part, as an expression of the conflict between these contradictions in policy.

Underestimation of Culture as a Political Variable

State policy has contributed to the strengthening of the indigenous movement in a third way. Historically, both policymakers and organizers of civil society have underestimated the potential of culture as a political force. The traditional left considered cultural diversity as something that would disappear with the impending unification of the working class. The state tended to accept cultural diversity as long as it did not appear to threaten the homogeneity of the political system. In Ecuador, for example, recent administrations have supported indigenous initiatives for bilingual educa-tion and other programs that were considered "cultural" and thus not a direct political threat. Yet, these programs facilitated the organization of indig-enous people based on their collective identity, which has contributed to the current ethnic unrest within the nation.

According to the government's perspective, the indigenous movement took advantage of a political opening. As Cynthia Enloe has stated, "The state not only responds to, but [also] can generate ethnic mobilization."[25] The Borja administration gave political legitimacy to CONAIE by opening negotiations with it, and the organization used that legitimacy to incite massive unrest. That legitimacy, coming from the government, was exactly the national political space that CONAIE needed to encourage increased support among the indigenous population. For the large indigenous popula-tion that considered itself to be disenfranchised by the Ecuadoran govern-ment, dialogue with the government represented a political voice. The 1990 Uprising, in turn, was a chance for the people to demonstrate that they were part of that voice and to demand that the voice of the indigenous people be heard — not only by the government but by all of Ecuadoran society. Government policies themselves had directly contributed to the increasing strength of indigenous organization in the country.

The organizing achievements of the indigenous people have pushed Ecuador's governments to react to societal pressure for a resolution of the problems of the indigenous population. Despite its internal problems, CONAIE is recognized internationally for its organizing successes. For example, CONAIE was instrumental in organizing the intercontinental campaign of "500 years of resistance," which protested the official celebration of the 500-year anniversary of the conquest of the Americas and united hundreds of indigenous organizations throughout the continent; CONAIE hosted the first intercontinental encounter in Quito in 1990. Such efforts have secured international recognition and support for CONAIE's political work in Ecuador.

An activist interviewed in Chimborazo explained the success of CONAIE as an organization that seeks to provide a social and political *alternative*, instead of simply pushing for reforms within the existing system. The movement, through its organizational process, finds itself confronted with a contradiction similar to that faced by the state. Just as the government is trying both to "democratize" and "modernize" (two goals that it has found contradictory), indigenous organizations are trying to promote respect for diversity and simultaneously demand equality within the Ecuadoran state. As explained by Alberto Melluci,

> The objective of the movement is not only equality of rights, but the right to be different. The struggle is against discrimination, and in favor of a more equitable distribution in the economic market; and, in the political realm, the struggle is still for citizenship. The right to be recognized as different is one of the deepest needs in post-industrial and post-material society.[26]

The work of the bilingual education projects over the last two decades has strengthened a consciousness of indigenous identity throughout the country, providing a social base upon which the indigenous organizations have been able to build. The movement is the result of long and continuing dialogue between the left and the indigenous movement. The focal point of this dialogue has been the relationship of social class to ethnic identity.

IDENTITY POLITICS AS A RESOURCE

Many of the people interviewed for this study, from government officials to organization leaders and isolated individuals, maintained that participation in the 1990 Uprising was extensive because the action was specifically indigenous. If the movement had been generalized for something more abstract such as "justice," or had been a mass strike, potential participants might not have felt that the Uprising responded to their specific situations and probably would not have taken to the streets.

In Ecuador, the indigenous movement is arguably the most viable popular movement. It has gained national and international political space, and in many cases an indigenous person is more likely to get land than a campesino. An apparent increase in the number of people who identify themselves as indigenous suggests that the concept is indeed fluid and can change with the situation. It has been pointed out that the concept of an indigenous identity itself is relatively new, coming from state categorization of the original inhabitants of the territory upon which it has been trying to forge a nation.[27] In this respect, indigenous identity can be seen as a "resource" mobilized for political objectives.

For a variety of reasons, it does appear that an increasing number of people identify themselves as indigenous. This is part of a larger continental, if not global, phenomenon that has both structural and ideological causes. The most recent census in the United States, for example, showed a dramatic increase in the number of people identifying themselves as indigenous. This can be explained partially by structural factors, in terms of the economic interests of the individual or, as is said in Spanish, "les conviene" (it suits them). Many jobs, fellowships, and other opportunities are available on a preferred basis to Native Americans in the United States.

This characterization of indigenous identity as a resource, though, must be recognized as an outcome of the political space won by successful organization of the indigenous movements throughout the hemisphere. An important ramification of the organizational process of indigenous people in Ecuador is the construction of a new collective identity. The fact that it is in their best interests to identify themselves as indigenous results from the gains made by mobilization based on collective identity and from the political space that is being won. The way in which this space is being won can best be demonstrated by returning to the specific case of the 1990 Uprising.

IMPACTS OF THE 1990 UPRISING

The 1990 Uprising was a manifestation of the process of reconstructing indigenous identity in the country, and its impact on Ecuadoran society is noticeable. Many observers posit that it stimulated an irreversible process of change in the social and political relations of the indigenous population in Ecuador. At the same time, it stimulated numerous new "investigations" by political and academic sources concerning the situation of indigenous people in Ecuador, which signifies that an important problem must be resolved. For CONAIE, the clearest gain from the 1990 Uprising is the political space it has won. Although, as mentioned previously, the Borja administration had taken steps toward responding to indigenous concerns, indigenous organizations were not considered equal participants in the process of resolving those issues; and society as a whole was not involved. The indigenous question now is of national and even international political importance for Ecuador.

The organizers of the 1990 Uprising, and, in most areas, its participants claim a large degree of success in terms of their political objectives. Most feel that the mobilization gave them a higher degree of dignity and respect because they demonstrated to the rest of the society their ability to organize and their importance to the economy of the country. Indigenous people claim that they have been better attended to in shops and in government offices since the 1990 Uprising. Some groups, however, particularly indigenous groups that oppose CONAIE, have claimed that the Uprising damaged their image. An evangelical indigenous community leader stated, "Our dignity as indigenous people was lowered because there was much theft.... Our personality as indigenous people has been criticized because of the robberies that took place in other communities."[28]

Even those groups that did not participate actively in the 1990 Uprising know that their complaints have been heard throughout the country and are, in fact, being discussed by the government. Ecuadorans in general, and government officials in particular, have publicly recognized the fact that Ecuador is a pluri-national country. Former President Borja even began to use the term "pluri-national" in his discourse.[29]

A second important political objective achieved was the stimulation of the organization process. Many communities that took part in the mass demonstrations were exposed to the indigenous organizations for the first time and later joined them, becoming formally organized. The number of land conflicts reported to IERAC have increased substantially, and regional organizations have increased their membership dramatically, as measured by the number of delegates at the assemblies of the organizations. Another important organizational benefit of the 1990 Uprising, described in a number of interviews, was that disputes between communities were resolved by the experience of working together during the Uprising. The two Saraguro organizations worked together, for example, as did competing organizations in Chimborazo, Imbabura, and elsewhere.

Not all of the objectives of the 1990 Uprising were met, however. Many land disputes remain unresolved, and negotiations with the government continue to be irregular. Overall, the gains were primarily symbolic, which in many instances has frustrated various communities. CONAIE itself became subject to the relative deprivation problem of trying to meet the expectations of the many communities that began to expect it to resolve their problems. At the community level, political organizing occurs primarily around specific issues, such as education and infrastructure. These issues may be least likely to realize immediate benefit from symbolic gains, such as political space or the reconstruction of identity. CONAIE's focus on issues of identity and symbolic power may have meant that the organization was less able to respond to local material needs.

The 1990 Uprising has also had a fundamental negative impact: increased military presence in the indigenous communities, particularly in the rural areas. Other negative impacts include retaliation against indigenous communities by large landowners and the formation of armed landowner "self-defense" units. Increased military presence in many communities and along the highways persisted for a sustained period after the 1990 Uprising. People complained of military searches in their residences and "spies" at meetings. Interestingly, the media gave little coverage to the increased military presence, but witnesses described it.

Since the 1990 Uprising, the military has taken steps to gain popularity within the indigenous communities by performing social services such as cleaning public spaces, building recreational facilities, and painting. The sudden intrusion of the military into the communities provoked numerous radio debates concerning the issue on indigenous broadcasts.[30] In some cases, military professionals have forcibly replaced indigenous teachers, according to reports from communities. Nevertheless, it remains unlikely that a military confrontation will develop in Ecuador as long as the government continues to attempt to address the issue of indigenous rights, which was on the national political agenda prior to 1990 and has been addressed as a much higher priority item ever since the Uprising.

INDIGENOUS MOVEMENT AS SOCIAL MOVEMENT

Theorists of social movements have shifted from grievance-oriented discussions of social upheavals toward the pursuit of a more elaborate understanding of the interactions involved in the fluctuating relationships of power in society. Escobar and Álvarez describe the process as follows, "Social action is understood as the product of complex social processes in which structure and agency interact in manifold ways and in which actors produce meanings, negotiate, and make decisions."[31]

A social movement becomes involved in the construction of collective identity because as it organizes, it defines itself as a social group to society and to its members. According to resource mobilization theorists, a strong collective identity is an important resource for collective action. Ethnic movements, including indigenous movements, are organized around such a collective identity. For the indigenous movement, collective identity is both a resource and the very reason for collective action. As mentioned earlier, the indigenous movement is involved both in the construction of collective identity and in demands for justice for the group, including, in this case, a broader concept of citizenship that will allow indigenous participation in the political system.

The indigenous movement in Ecuador has organized around identity as indigenous people and has won a political space for a sector of society that was traditionally excluded from national politics. Because of the importance of that political space for rural people, the indigenous movement has become a political voice for them — an alternative to identifying themselves as campesinos, workers, or members of political party organizations. The massive participation in the 1990 Uprising demonstrated that, at least in that moment, people felt a strong alignment with indigenous identity, and thus, with the indigenous movement.

In the case of the indigenous communities, ethnic identity is fluid. Because the society is largely mestizo, members of indigenous communities, as long as they know the national language, can "transculturate" and hide or give up their indigenous identity. However, for political, economic, or social reasons, they can just as easily maintain indigenous identity; and they also can go back and forth. Indigenous identity is ascriptive. Thus, when ethnic identity is fluid, the choice of identity responds to both structural and ideological social factors.

Indigenous communities are reshaping what is conceived of as political space and are influencing the societal conception of indigenous people in the process. Like social movements elsewhere, they organize to meet their political needs when the national government fails to respond; using these methods, they have been able to carve out a new political space for themselves both in political struggles with the government and in their ever-changing relationship with society.

CONCLUSIONS

The subject of indigenous rights is now a permanent part of the national political agenda in Ecuador. Direct confrontation with indigenous issues in the political arena may influence the state to redefine its nation-building goal, which would minimize the contradictions between nation building and democracy building, and thus would potentially minimize violence.

The indigenous movement in Ecuador represents the plural nature of Ecuadoran society, and the movement demands that the government respond to it accordingly. Perhaps more than other social movements, the indigenous movement challenges the hierarchical forms of political organization and domination because the movement inherently represents premodern forms of organization, although it functions effectively in a postmodern world. The structure of the indigenous federation is pluralistic, interacting with various indigenous cultures and traditional forms of representation. Simultaneously, the federation is forging unity based on a common experience of discrimination against "Indians."

Unlike other social movements in Latin America, the indigenous movement represents the most excluded sector of these societies. Its main political resource has been indigenous identity, which has been mobilized for use as a political tool. By mobilizing effectively around collective ethnic identity as indigenous people, the movement has succeeded in winning political space for itself in Ecuador, as has occurred in other places throughout the continent. Ironically, indigenous people, the sector considered the most conservative and backward-looking by the left and considered the most passive by the society's dominant culture has proved to be one of the strongest forces for democratic change today.

The indigenous movement in Ecuador is both a "new social movement" based on identity and a form of collective action based on resource mobilization. This analysis of the indigenous 1990 Uprising in Ecuador demonstrates that these are complementary, not contradictory, perspectives. Identity is the most important resource the indigenous population has. Considering their exclusion as indigenous people from national politics, identity might even be considered their only political resource. While the struggle for political space for indigenous people has enjoyed some successes, it is important to note that material gains are not as easily observed. Strategic moves by CONAIE may be focused more on gaining political access than on meeting the material needs of the indigenous communities; this could become a structural weakness and could lead to diminishing popular support for the movement over time. This is also a contradiction within identity-based movements that the indigenous movement in Ecuador has yet to resolve. Future analysis of social movements in Latin America must consider the political significance of identity-based political movements as well as the political, social, and economic situations that benefit or constrain them.

Their cultural survival despite 500 years of various forms of colonization gives indigenous people a strong base around which to organize what can be seen as a counter-hegemonic force. Observers have noted the failure of the Ecuadoran state to become hegemonic as a nation-state. The political mobilization of cultural distinction by the indigenous organizations may encourage the Ecuadoran government to accept a new relationship between the state and civil society. The search for new relationships of this kind has become increasingly important, as ethnic conflicts have flared recently within nation-states throughout the world. The many politically excluded groups in Ecuadoran society are becoming increasingly organized into social movements like the indigenous movement.[32] The next few decades may see the continued democratization of the Ecuadoran state in light of the plurality that exists in that society. The 1990 Uprising began a new phase of indigenous politics in Ecuador. The list of demands CONAIE presented to the government (see Appendix 4) constituted the first time the indigenous movement had presented a united, written platform. Participants were using their newly developed resources: literacy and contemporary indigenous ideology. Chapter 5 will examine the use of these tools.

Notes

1. There is relevant debate concerning whether more types of protest actually exist, or analysts have merely begun to consider types of protest that have always been present. See Alberto Melluci, 1984, "An End to Social Movements?" *Social Science Information* 23 (4/5): 819-835; and Scott 1985.

2. Jean Cohen, 1985, "Strategy or Identity," *Social Research* 52: 4 (Winter).

3. Antonio Gramsci, 1971, *Selections from the Prison Notebooks of Antonio Gramsci* (New York: International).

4. For analysis of this process, refer to José Sánchez Parga, 1993, *Transformaciones culturales y educación indígena* (Quito: Centro Andino de Acción Popular — CAAP); Juan Botasso, ed., 1986, *Del Indigenismo a las organizaciones* indígenas (Quito: Abya-Yala); and Roberto Santana, 1995, *Ciudadanos en la Etnicidad: Los indios en la política o la política de los indios* (Quito: Abya-Yala). Or, for the perspective of the organizations themselves, see CONAIE, 1989, *Las nacionalidades indígenas en el Ecuador: Nuestro proceso organizativo* (Quito: Abya-Yala).

5. For a useful review of trends in social movement theory in Latin America, see the introduction in Arturo Escobar and Sonia Álvarez, eds., 1992, *The Making of Social Movements in Latin America* (Boulder, Colo.: Westview Press).

6. See Segundo Moreno Yánez and José Figueroa, 1992, *El Levantamiento Indígena del Inti-Raymi* (Quito: Abya-Yala), 68.

7. Moreno and Figueroa 1992, 73.

8. See Sánchez Parga, 1993, and Botero, 1992, for different perspectives on the land question as it relates to the political movement.

9. Macas, 1993, interview by author.

10. Macas, 1993, interview by author.

11. Jorge León, 1994, *De campesinos a ciudadanos diferentes* (Quito: CEDIME — Centro de Investigaciones de los Movimientos Sociales del Ecuador), 17.

12. Elizabeth Jelin, 1990, *Women and Social Change in Latin America* (London: United Nations Research Institute and Zed Books), 206.

13. Interview by author with a leader of the Federación Indígena de Imbabura.

14. Macas, 1993, interview by author.

15. Roxanne Dunbar Ortiz, 1984, *Indians of the Americas: Human Rights and Self-Determination* (London: Zed Press), 108.

16. Luis Macas, 1991, "El Levantamiento Indígena visto por sus protagonistas," in *INDIOS: Una reflexión sobre el Levantamiento Indígena de 1990*, ed. Diego Cornejo Menacho (Quito: Logos), 28.

17. Ortiz, 1991, interview by author.

18. Luis Macas, 1991, interview by author; and Humberto Muenala, 1991, interview by author.

19. Luna, 1991, interview by author.

20. Macas, 1991, interview by author.

21. Ted R. Gurr, 1969, *Why Men Rebel* (Princeton, N.J.: Princeton University Press), 24.

22. For discussion of social movements in Latin America, see Escobar and Álvarez 1992; Susan Eckstein, ed., 1989, *Power and Popular Protest* (Berkeley, Calif.: University of California Press); and Gerardo Munck, 1991, "Social Movements and Democracy in Latin America: Theoretical Debates and Comparative Perspectives," a paper for the April Latin American Studies Association (LASA) conference.

23. Luis Luna Gaybor, 1991, director of IERAC (Instituto Ecuatoriano de Reforma Agraria y Colonización), interview by author.

24. See Anderson 1983 for a critical discussion of the construction of national identity.

25. Cynthia Enloe, 1981, "The Growth of the State and Ethnic Mobilization," *Ethnic and Racial Studies* 4 (2): 124.

26. Alberto Melucci, 1984, "An End to Social Movements?" *Social Science Information* 23 (4/5), 830-831. Melucci is discussing feminism here, but the concept is relevant for ethnic-based social movements as well.

27. Cynthia Enloe 1981, describes this process.

28. Federación de Cabildos de Cacha, 1991, interview by author. The reference is to the theft from produce trucks that tried to pass the blockades in some isolated areas. Those actions were condemned by the organizations. It is interesting to note that the main evangelical indigenous organization, Center for the Investigation of Indigenous Education (Centro de Investigaciones para la Educación Indígena — CIEI), participated in the 1997 and 2000 mobilizations.

29. Ortiz, 1991, interview by author.

30. Miguel Lluco, 1991, ECUARUNARI leader from Chimborazo, interview by author.

31. Escobar and Álvarez, 1992, 4.

32. See the work of Amy Lind, 1995, "Gender Development and Women's Political Practices in Ecuador" (Ph.D. diss., Cornell University), on the women's movement in Ecuador, for example. There is also growing literature on the Afro-Ecuadoran sector.

Chapter 5

The Politics of Identity Reconstruction

INTRODUCTION

This chapter will demonstrate how the indigenous movement in Ecuador is challenging the meaning of citizenship and democratic participation through the framework of the distinct indigenous identity. This analysis complements a growing body of literature concerning identity-based movements in Latin America, but it carries the discussion further into the actual political ramifications of identity movements in Latin America. How do they affect the political system? Is identity an effective way for civil society to organize? In the case of Ecuador, the indigenous organizations, while struggling for apparently sectarian concerns, actually constitute one of the strongest forces for the opening of the country's democratic system.

The following pages will briefly examine 1) the indigenous political response to modernization of agricultural production and 2) the political struggle for bilingual indigenous education in Ecuador. Analysis of these two issues will elucidate some ways in which the indigenous movement has affected the political process. In both cases, I contend, the demands of indigenous leaders have been focused on participation. Indigenous leaders insist that their perspectives should be included in development plans for their lands and environment. The centrality of participation as a demand demonstrates the context of exclusion in which the indigenous movement developed.

Indigenous people have gained few positions and count on few allies within the state; yet, they have succeeded in winning a political space for themselves in both national and local politics. They have brought their issues firmly into the political agenda. This has been achieved partly through demonstrations of organizational capability, as in the unprecedented Indigenous Uprising that dramatically affected commerce in the country in 1990, as discussed in Chapter 4, and partly through influencing society's general understanding of indigenous people. Indigenous intellectuals have permeated Ecuadoran society with an "indigenous ideology" that influences how members of the dominant mestizo culture perceive indigenous people as well as how indigenous people think about themselves. One of the most effective ways in which the ideology has been spread is through bilingual literacy campaigns and education. The process of teaching and legitimizing the indigenous languages also has allowed bilingual educators to inform the public about the reality of the indigenous condition. At the time of the 1990 Uprising, one statistical study showed, "There was a national consensus: Most Indians live in subhuman conditions, and it is the responsibility of all of Ecuadoran society to resolve this situation."[1]

This chapter begins with a discussion of the context of exclusion that created the setting for the cases that will be presented. A discussion follows of the development of what I call the "contemporary indigenous ideology," including reference to the "class versus ethnicity" debate and the actual precepts of the ideology. With this background established, the chapter concludes with two cases of indigenous political intervention: the first, their fight for bilingual, bicultural education, and the second, their response to plans for economic reform in the agricultural sector.

A CONTEXT OF EXCLUSION

Exclusion of indigenous peoples is cultural, economic, and political. Exclusion is cultural in the sense that a colonialist mentality of Spanish domination of indigenous peoples laid the foundation for the development of a European-style nation-state that would include economic and political integration as well as projects of forced cultural assimilation. Indigenous models of societal organization were considered inferior to European models, and the indigenous people, likewise, were considered inferior. The resulting relationship was one of cultural domination. This history still influences the views of many political authorities. A high-ranking political representative of one province said in an interview, "The reason Ecuador is so poor is that we have too many Indians."[2]

Ecuador's colonial history also led to economic exclusion of indigenous people. Agrarian reform in the 1960s and 1970s gave the indigenous population of the Highlands region a reprieve from semifeudal agrarian structures such as the *encomienda* and *huasipungo*, the Ecuadoran form of indentured servitude or sharecropping. Large landholdings still dominate the Highlands' economy, however, and shortage of land due to demographic pressures continues to place immense economic and social strain on local communities. Small farmers (primarily indigenous) control only 30 percent of cultivatable land in this region.[3]

In the Amazon, agrarian reform had a different impact on indigenous communities. The 1964 Agrarian Reform Law included "as a national urgent priority the colonization of the Amazon region."[4] As a response to unequal land distribution and demographic pressures in the Highlands, the government gave land titles to settlers who cleared and produced on land that was considered vacant. Vacant land was defined as that which had "remained uncultivated for more than 10 consecutive years."[5] Unfortunately, much of the colonized land was indigenous territory, a part of the complex indigenous system of "foresting," or living with the land in an ecologically sound manner without permanent clear-cutting of forests. Thus, while some indigenous communities in the Highlands gained land titles through agrarian reform, the net result for indigenous people in the Amazon was a loss of territory.

Economic and cultural exclusion has reinforced the political exclusion of indigenous people that prevails in Ecuador. Indigenous participation in representative political positions, while having increased during the past 20 years, is extremely limited. This low level of participation has become a central issue of the contemporary indigenous platform. Indigenous leaders contend that the current system is a foreign one that does not respect indigenous cultures and barely acknowledges their existence. As Ampam Karakras, a Shuar intellectual explained, "The Constitution and the laws do not represent our aspirations, nor are they meant to, but those of an unjust society, a different society, culture, politics, structure, and laws that do not correspond to our reality."[6] A local indigenous leader from Bolívar province made a similar observation in simpler terms, when asked what he wanted from the government: "That they consider that we are also a part of the state and we have rights just like everyone else, which we are now demanding."[7]

Indigenous activists routinely state that the Ecuadoran nation-state does not represent them, and until it does, they believe they have the right to challenge its legitimacy. CONAIE officially boycotted the electoral process until the 1996 elections. "It was a way to reject the invalidity of a system of government that does not represent the Ecuadoran people; it doesn't recognize the ethnic groups that exist in the country."[8]

In Ecuador, the illiterate, which includes most of the indigenous population, were allowed to vote for the first time in the post-military regime elections of 1979.[9] Although indigenous people were legally freed from service tenure in 1964, they were not yet free of their impoverished condition in the agricultural sector, as is discussed below. The nation-building project that included teaching Spanish to the indigenous population in an attempt at cultural integration was contradicted by the socioeconomic separation of the indigenous people from the Spanish-speaking population. The contemporary indigenous movement capitalizes on the context of exclusion to strengthen the identity of indigenous peoples.

FINDING A VOICE: THE DEVELOPMENT OF AN INDIAN IDEOLOGY

When a university student, an intellectual in Quito, a bilingual school teacher in the countryside, and an Amazonian hunter-gatherer all respond in the same way to a question about their indigenous identity, this suggests that they share a similar political ideology. Ideology signifies "the ideas and beliefs that symbolize the conditions and life experience of a specific, socially significant group or class."[10] The above-mentioned individuals live in very different contexts and have diverse material needs, but because they are indigenous, they all experience discrimination. When asked, for example, what was the main issue of the 1990 Uprising, they all answered, "Dignity." The shared ideology, or understanding of their condition, results from the evolution of contemporary organizing, political debate, and the process of obtaining bilingual adult literacy and bilingual education. Out of the land struggles in the countryside during the 1970s and 1980s, an indigenous movement emerged that defined itself as characteristically different from the traditional left.

CLASS AND ETHNICITY

The discussion in Ecuador about class and ethnicity is a microcosm of the historical discussion among Marxist and post-Marxist scholars and activists about the limits of class-based analysis for understanding modern social movements. To summarize, traditional Marxist theory tries to de-emphasize ethnic or nationalist forms of organization, suggesting that economic modernization will soon cause those categories to be subsumed by economic class. Post-Marxists[11] contend that society will remain segregated and that analysts must look for new paradigms to explain social movement politics.

In Ecuador, the indigenous movement shifted during the 1970s and 1980s from class-based to identity-based organizations. Indigenous activists say they began organizing around land conflicts, peasant-based organizations aligned with leftist parties, and groups whose main demands were related to the agrarian reform process. Through the organizing process, they discovered that specific needs such as bilingual education and the problems of discrimination were not being addressed within other organizations. "Our situation remained isolated in the syndicalist organizations," explained Maria Paca, an activist from Chimborazo, "so we formed . . . our own organization as indigenous people, looking for the needs of indigenous peoples."[12]

Ethnic identity is an important example of the many social identities around which contemporary movements continue to organize. While early theories of ethnicity regarded it as "primordial," or something into which people are born, and even biological, as regards race, debates about ethnicity have evolved somewhat, though the issues still are far from being resolved. More recent literature recognizes a situational aspect of ethnic identity. This is particularly significant in Latin America, where a history of racial mixing has made the lines between ethnic groups less clearly defined in some areas than in others. In this region, ethnicity is usually "defined in social and cultural, not biological terms."[13]

Usually, one ethnic group in a society holds a dominant position because it shares the ethnic identity of the hegemonic power. This discriminatory relationship reproduces ethnic antagonisms. "We are both exploited, the Indian and the worker, but the worker has a higher social status than the Indian, so workers have the privilege of laughing at Indians," explained Luis Macas, past president of CONAIE.[14]

According to Alicia Ibarra, leftist intellectuals, during the agrarian reform period of the 1960s and 1970s, saw the Ecuadoran state as a tool of capitalist development, while intellectuals who focused on ethnicity, often young indigenous scholars and anthropologists, were more likely to see the state as defending a dominant culture rather than a dominant economic class.[15]

Differences such as these became evident not only in discourse, but also in the actual organization process. Mass strikes that may win power for labor in a workers' conflict may be inappropriate in a land struggle; and while indigenous communities supported workers' strikes during the 1970s, they found that they did not receive reciprocal solidarity from the left in land struggles.[16] The position of the left-wing parties was that the indigenous groups would join the working class. A leader of the MPD stated, for example: "The central problem (in Ecuador) is not a racial one, but a class problem, and that is how we should approach it to find the best solution."[17]

Eventually, it became evident that the indigenous movement needed to develop its own strategies, although it has retained many strategic elements from the traditional left.[18] No evidence shows that indigenous organizations in Ecuador ever have been involved in armed resistance, and it is inaccurate to categorize indigenous groups as "the left" because their ideology differs from, and they generally attempt to distinguish their positions from, those of leftist parties.[19]

In the 1970s, while the workers' movement was at its high point and the first indigenous youth were attending college, the left had a fairly direct influence on indigenous communities. In order to launch indigenous candidates, for the most part in provincial or cantonal elections, indigenous individuals sometimes affiliated with parties such as the Ecuadoran Socialist Party (Partido Socialista Ecuatoriano — PSE), the Popular Democratic Movement Party (Movimiento Popular Democrático — MPD), or the Broad

Leftist Front (Frente Amplio de Izquierda — FADI).[20] This became important in 1979, when indigenous people voted for the first time. Especially in the Highlands, young indigenous intellectuals were influenced by the left, as were other youths in Ecuador.

Throughout the tenuous alliance with the left, indigenous peoples debated the efficacy of workers' organizations and leftist parties to resolve specific problems of the indigenous population. For example, in one of the first land takeovers, which took place in Chimborazo province in 1988, indigenous people who supported FADI began to farm on the fallow lands of a hacienda, but after a month they were dislocated by indigenous MPD supporters who had an allegiance to the landowner. According to one participant, the dispute between the leftist political parties led to divisions among the indigenous communities themselves.[21]

As indigenous students began to discuss bilingual education, they challenged the Marxist belief that cultural differences would somehow disappear. Their challenge was threatening to some established indigenous groups who held with a class-based ideology, groups such as the Federation of Indigenous Evangelicals (Federación Ecuatoriana de Indígenas Evangélicos — FEINE), which was formed in 1944 with the support of the Communist Party. "There was not a strong identification with 'Indian-ness' (*lo indígena*) in the Sierra organizations, although their roots were all [in] indigenous identity. Any other movement that wanted to emerge, in this case the indigenous movement, was considered racist, separatist, and divisive."[22] As the traditional left began to lose power in Ecuador in the 1980s, older class-based organizations such as ECUARUNARI, the largest indigenous federation representing the Highlands, began to adopt more of the indigenous identity-based ideology that was developing in the countryside and among intellectuals.

How did one of the most important social movements in Ecuador come to be based on ethnic identity?[23] The first and most obvious explanation concerns the cultural heritage of the population. Despite the nation-building process in Ecuador, indigenous people continue to perceive themselves as excluded from receiving most social and political benefits of the modern state. This exclusion contributes to a sense of "otherness" in the large indigenous population of Ecuador. In other words, the hegemonic project of the state has not been successful in Ecuador.[24] Using a Gramscian framework, we can understand the attempt at nation building in Ecuador as the hegemonic project of the modernizing state. The indigenous movement, with its alternative perspectives on culture and society, presents a counter-hegemonic movement. Two factors even more specific to the Ecuadoran case contribute to the importance of identity politics there. For the present discussion, although the labels are simplifications, let us call these the "Amazonian ethnonationalist factor" and the "upward mobility factor."

The Amazonian ethnonationalist factor has been extremely influential in the development of indigenous organizations in Ecuador. The Shuar Federation, formed in the early 1960s and representing about 45,000 Shuar people in the southern Amazonian region of Ecuador, probably was the first ethnonationalist indigenous organization in the region. Formed with the help of Salesian (Italian) missionaries who wanted to protect the Shuar's and their own landholdings, the Shuar Federation has maintained a fiercely independent nature and has focused on economic development for the Shuar nation. When young Shuar students began to study at universities in Quito (in the Highlands), they brought with them their experience of organizing independently as an indigenous people. The Amazon region, because of its isolation from the centers of the country, has had a separate process of development; indigenous communities there are less integrated into the nation, and many do not speak Spanish. In addition, the Amazonian influence appears to have greatly influenced existing indigenous organizations of the Sierra, groups such as the FEI, which were formed earlier with the support of the political left.[25]

The second, upward mobility factor has to do with the transforming socioeconomic situation of indigenous individuals. Increasingly, indigenous people have found ways to improve their economic standing without sacrificing their cultural distinctiveness. The most celebrated example of this phenomenon is found in the province of Imbabura, where many of the indigenous people of Otavalo (*otavaleños*) are experiencing a tremendous economic success story. These people traditionally were travelers and traders throughout the Andean region. Through the international marketing of their textiles and other products, as well as their traditional music, some have gained an economic independence that has allowed them to sustain a strong cultural independence. Their success also allowed for the emergence of some of the first "organic intellectuals" of Ecuador's indigenous movement. Most indigenous people in Imbabura still live in impoverished conditions, but enough have been able to achieve economic success, while maintaining a strong identity, to have had a strong influence in the region a whole. The cultural independence of the *otavaleños* of Imbabura increasingly contributes to their political strength.

Upward mobility has important ramifications for the relationship between ethnicity and class in Ecuador. The Otavalo case is only one example among an increasing number of indigenous groups whose economic successes have reinforced their cultural distinctiveness. This development has changed socioeconomic relations in some communities so much that the common theory linking transculturation to upward mobility is no

*The Otavalo people have improved their economic standing
without sacrificing their culture.*

longer adequate. Belote and Belote have argued that indigenous people in
Latin America historically have been encouraged by the economic elite to
become a part of the dominant culture in order to find economic success
within it. But when indigenous communities have had economic successes,
they are no longer obliged to sacrifice their culture in order to survive. In
some cases, maintaining indigenous identity has even been beneficial to the
improvement of an individual's social class.[26]

THE IDENTITY-BASED IDEOLOGY

The indigenous movement in Ecuador can be said to have shifted from
class based to identity based, but it never was divorced from the struggle
for land. Land is usually at the center of any indigenous movement because
it is an integral part of cultural reproduction as well as an economic
necessity. The issue of land brought together the two divergent perspectives
of the indigenous movement of the early 1980s, according to Miguel Ángel
Carlosamán, a leader of the movement:

> "There were two visions: the indigenous cultural vision, focused on bilingual
> education, and the class vision, focused on land conflicts. The two merged when
> we realized that we could not have our culture without land."[27]

The vision that has emerged is still developing with the changing
political context, but it contributed to the framework of the ideology upon
which today's indigenous movement is based. In order to present an
overview of what the ideology encompasses, I will refer to the political
platform of CONAIE, the prominent indigenous confederation.

The CONAIE platform has evolved to include not only the resolution of land conflicts, but also specific political demands on the Ecuadoran state. In general, the movement demands that indigenous people be treated as "equal but different." Ecuadoran sociologist Jorge León has categorized the demands of the indigenous movement into three areas: ethnic, class, and citizenship.[28] Following this general typology, the CONAIE's platform will be summarized below in parallel terms of culture, economy, and political policy.[29]

In the arena of culture, the work of CONAIE revolves primarily around educational issues because that is where the government directly intervenes in cultural reproduction. The political implications of bilingual education are discussed extensively below. The main demand is for bilingual, intercultural education with guaranteed funding, administered by indigenous people. CONAIE has also suggested that the Spanish-speaking population should be required to study an indigenous language.

In the area of economics, CONAIE demands allocation of funding for the resolution of land conflicts and immediate resolution of the conflicts. This is an issue because of inefficiencies in the land redistribution program. For example, the government's National Agrarian Development Institute (Instituto Nacional de Desarrollo Agrario — INDA)[30] may rule in favor of a community and against a landowner in a conflict but then fail to provide the necessary funds for the community to buy the lands in a timely manner. Some cases remain unresolved for many years, and this, in turn, can lead to violent conflicts.

Another constant demand directly from the Highlands communities is for price controls on agricultural inputs, such as fertilizers, and protection of prices for agricultural products. Other economic issues include the establishment of funds for indigenous development and the repatriation of some profits from the oil industry to the Amazonian indigenous communities.

CONAIE's most controversial and publicized policy demand is for the Constitution to recognize Ecuador as a pluri-national, pluri-cultural country. This demand is extremely important because it conceivably could give the indigenous communities rights as "different" citizens, that is, specific rights as spelled out by the UN Human Rights Convention corresponding to their needs as "peoples" with cultures. Additionally, it represents acceptance by the government and, tacitly, by Ecuadoran society of the main tenet of indigenous ideology: Indigenous people are here to stay.[31] The CONAIE definition is as follows:

> Pluri-national State: Is the organization of government that represents the joint political, economic, and social power of the peoples and nationalities of a country: that is, the Pluri-national State is formed when various peoples and nationalities unite under the same government, directed by a Constitution. This is distinct from the present Uni-national State that only represents the dominant sectors. [32]

In the constitutional reforms of 1998, Ecuador declared itself a pluri-national state. Prior to that declaration, the Ecuadoran government and the Ecuadoran mestizo elite were threatened by this concept because it challenged their legitimacy as the dominant culture; and they argued against it on grounds that it would divide an already small nation. Former President Osvaldo Hurtado gave the following comment on the issue of nation building: "To speak of an Ecuador of many nationalities would not help the objective that all Ecuadorans should strive toward, which is to build a unified nation."[33] Although the degree of desired autonomy varies among communities, indigenous people never proposed to divide Ecuador. Instead, they aimed to challenge the government to reflect the diversity of society and to renovate the system and make it more open to participation. The former president of CONAIE, Luis Macas, explained, "Bit by bit, the indigenous movement has developed qualitatively its struggle, its proposals. Before, it was a struggle for survival, for land, for defense and recuperation of territories. Today it is a political proposal, and it is a proposal for all of society."[34]

Interestingly, while some indigenous groups and individuals oppose CONAIE, their ideologies are noticeably similar. Alberto Andrango is a leader of the National Federation of Campesino Organizations (FENOC), a campesino/indigenous organization affiliated with a workers' union that has a strong following only in its home canton of Cotocachi, with small affiliates in other provinces. FENOC, which is considered to be class-based, has criticized CONAIE for being too "culturalist"; yet, when asked about the objectives of forming FENOC, Andrango replied, "Against discrimination . . . the first point was respect for indigenous people."[35] Similarly, José Quimbo, President Durán's advisor on indigenous affairs, was engaged in a bitter political rivalry with CONAIE, but when asked about his objectives while in his presidential office, he said that just by being in the palace, he was winning the ruling elite's respect for indigenous people.[36] Both Andrango and Quimbo agreed with CONAIE that Ecuador is a pluri-national country, although they hesitated, knowing that the term is associated with CONAIE.

Interviews conducted throughout Ecuador in the early 1990s suggested that indigenous communities and other sympathetic sectors of society had adopted the ideology CONAIE promotes. Some discrepancy may still exist between the language of intellectual leaders and the needs expressed in local communities, but there is a general understanding of the conditions and goals of Ecuador's indigenous people. These people define themselves as nationalities that deserve respect and the same rights as mestizos, without having to sacrifice their distinctive cultures.

The political vision based in indigenous culture and identity is linked directly to the bilingual education movement. The movement for bilingual education instilled pride in indigenous culture while simultaneously creating a generation of leaders within indigenous communities who promote contemporary indigenous ideology. An academic analysis of the literacy campaign states, "Eventually, as a result of the education of the bases, we were generating young leadership for the organizations."[37] The movement was led by young indigenous intellectuals who sparked a bilingual literacy project designed to promote native languages. Since colonial times, bilingual education had been a method for teaching indigenous children Spanish and thus integrating them into the dominant mestizo culture. The new generation of indigenous leaders changed the objective to one of maintaining diverse languages. They took pride in their culture and tried to encourage pride among their communities. They urged indigenous communities to fight back against the discrimination that made them ashamed to be Indians. The issue of discrimination hit home among members of the communities, and with discrimination leading the list of issues, indigenous organizing flourished.

POLITICS OF IDENTITY: BILINGUAL EDUCATION

The first bilingual literacy campaigns, during the 1970s and early 1980s, were instrumental in the political formation of the current crop of indigenous leaders. The individuals trained in these programs became the conveyors of the new indigenous ideology. They concurrently became political actors, both because of their involvement in the empowerment of

Bilingual intercultural education students

their communities and through their demands for changes in the national educational system. "Above all, it was through the adult literacy program that our organization was consolidated," one provincial leader explained.[38] Literacy campaigns were supported as a means to help disenfranchised indigenous people become informed political actors. The political battles over education climaxed in 1988, when an accord between CONAIE and the Ministry of Education and Culture established the National Directorate of Bilingual Intercultural Education (Dirección Nacional de Educación Intercultural Bilingüe — DINEIB), which oversees bilingual schools throughout the country.

The bilingual education movement appears to have its roots in the radio literacy programs run by evangelical church groups in the Amazon, particularly the Summer Institute of Linguistics (SIL) and the progressive evangelical church of Monsignor Leonidas Proaño in the Highlands. Radio is a major form of communication and news among indigenous populations because of rural geographic conditions and illiteracy. The radio programs have taught indigenous people basic literacy using their own languages, although the goal of the Proaño project was integration into the Spanish/ mestizo culture. In contrast, an innovative literacy project by the Center for the Investigation of Indigenous Education (CIEI), based at the Pontifical Catholic University of Ecuador (Pontificia Universidad Católica del Ecuador), trained indigenous people to teach Quichua literacy in the communities with the objective of language retention.

The CIEI program was innovative in that it intended to promote, rather than diminish, Quichua usage, and it represented a dramatic change in government policy toward the language. The CIEI was supported by an agreement with the Ministry of Education and Culture during the Roldós-Hurtado administrations (1979-1984). Within the indigenous movement, the project was controversial. Some of the more Marxist-influenced leaders argued that it was bourgeois to focus on education instead of the material struggle for land. Although directed by a *mestiza* (mestizo woman), the project was staffed almost entirely by indigenous students. According to the CIEI director, the university community balked. The university administration tried to impede the flow of funds, and Hispanic students even organized a strike to "express their rejection of so many Indians entering the University."[39]

The main projects of the CIEI were to train community educators to teach adult literacy in indigenous communities and to develop a curriculum for bilingual, bicultural education. The center made a political decision to begin with adult literacy because, according to indigenous educator Humberto Muenala, "We needed our adults to be an example to our children, so first we had to win them back."[40] Illiteracy in the countryside is four times higher than in the cities, and it is highest in the central Andes, where the indigenous population is the densest.[41] Workshops were held to train literate indigenous adults, delegated by their community organizations to be instructors. More than 1,000 educators returned to their communities during the 1980-1984 period with CIEI didactic materials. By involving adults from the beginning, the program was able to achieve its other objective: the strengthening of cultural identity.

Beyond the goal of promoting literacy, the content of literacy instruction materials was structured to encourage students to resolve practical problems they faced. In one book, for instance, they were asked where they should go to complain if they did not have electricity or potable water in their community. If they did not know the answer, it was discussed, and in that way they were empowered to take action that previously they might have been too shy or uninformed to pursue. For example, a trainer might ask students, "Where would you go to ask for potable water?" If the class did not know, the teacher took them on a field trip to the municipal authorities and showed them the administrative and political procedures necessary to obtain potable water. The experience also was used to teach the students that they have a right to clean water and that the government has the obligation to provide it to them.[42] Along with practical lessons in literacy and local political processes, the students learned to value their language, and along with it, their culture. In a country where only a decade before schoolchildren were forced to cut their braids and speak Spanish, this constituted a significant change.

Perhaps the most remarkable evidence of changing attitudes about the Quichua language was seen in 1980, when President-elect Jaime Roldós gave part of his inaugural address in Quichua, recognizing the indigenous contribution to his victory and promising to defend indigenous rights. Of course, this was the first time that indigenous people had voted en masse, as Roldós was well aware. The director of the CIEI noted that Roldós' speech was the first time a state authority had addressed the population in a language other than Spanish. This action represented the fruit of years of work to reestablish the value of indigenous languages and cultures. Both the dominant and the dominated groups have a new consciousness, although still relatively passive, about the importance and value of the indigenous languages spoken in the country.[43]

In other sectors, a realization of the importance of bilingual education was spreading, even among those indigenous organizations such as the CONAIE member organization from the Highlands, ECUARUNARI, whose Marxist leadership had caused suspicion of "bourgeois" indigenous intellectuals, including those who ran the literacy project.

The CIEI, along with the training of instructors, oversaw the opening of 300 rural bilingual-education schools with trained instructors, and illiteracy in Ecuador dropped from 25.7 percent in 1979 to 12.6 percent in 1984. Despite CIEI's successes, indigenous organizations claimed that it interfered with their direct control over bilingual education, and the fact that it was directed by a mestizo de-legitimized the center in their view. For instance, the ECUARUNARI criticized indigenous people who worked with the project for "selling out" because they were paid by the government.[44] A direct agreement between CONAIE and the Ministry of Education and Culture was reached at the end of 1988, during the government of Rodrigo Borja. This contract instituted DINEIB, which, although administered by the ministry, would be staffed by CONAIE.

The establishment of DINEIB was a triumph for the indigenous movement after many years of political struggle that included lobbying politicians as well as the massive occupation of the Ministry of Education and Culture. Besides the direct gains of the government's granting of legitimacy to bilingual education and to CONAIE, there was a broader political impact: The agreement, establishing DINEIB with its staffing controlled by CONAIE, made a dent in the clientelism that greatly impedes democratic systems in Ecuador, especially in the countryside. Clientelism was directly impacted by the shift in control over teachers in indigenous areas.

The schoolteacher often is one of the most important influences in an indigenous community and one of the few steady jobs in the countryside. Before the establishment of DINEIB, the task of assigning teaching positions was handled by the national representatives from each province through their party representatives. With the establishment of DINEIB, this task was delegated to the indigenous organizations affiliated with CONAIE. The first director of DINEIB, Luis Monteluisa, reported, "I saw in Napo province, for instance, that the provincial deputy [representative to Congress] named 80 percent of the teachers; the provincial director of education named 10 percent; and the party director, the other 10 percent. All of this power passed directly to the indigenous leaders."[45]

Through the clientelistic bargaining practice, political favors had been done, and votes had been guaranteed. Congressional representatives strongly opposed President Borja's proposition to relinquish this important local power to the "Indians." Monteluisa recalled, "Some people didn't even realize it, but others knew what it meant to administer education: There is power there."[46] Although public figures rarely expressed their disapproval openly for political reasons, President Borja's Democratic Left Party secretly threatened to boycott him if he actually went through with the agreement. Nevertheless, with political acumen and in spite of the pressure against it, Borja did uphold his agreement with CONAIE, thus institutionalizing CONAIE's influence throughout the country.[47]

DINEIB has been wracked by political and economic difficulties since its inception in 1988. In some cases, clientelism has not been eradicated, but simply transferred to a different social sector. The regional indigenous organizations (as members of CONAIE) did not always choose the most technically effective candidates for administrative positions, but sometimes chose the ones most loyal to the organization. Similarly, many teachers are activists with the organization, and they miss an unacceptable number of school days in order to attend political events.[48] While these problems are being addressed through a process of self-evaluation, the politicized nature of the bilingual education program appears to be interfering with some aspects of its implementation. Despite the literacy and education programs, the use of the Quichua language continues to drop at an alarming rate.[49]

DINEIB now is a permanent institution within the Ministry of Education and Culture. The indigenous organizations consider this an important political triumph. Early in his administration, when President Durán (1992-1996) attempted to dismantle CONAIE's control of the directorate, he met with mass protests and public criticism. In a press release about the attempted changes, CONAIE stated that "the Ecuadoran government is putting in serious danger the rights of the indigenous peoples of the country."[50] The dramatic dismantling was halted, but negotiations continued within the ministry to modify the bilingual education system.

DINEIB remains a public affirmation not only of the continued survival of indigenous cultures, but also of the concrete political space that assures the continued promotion of indigenous ideology at community and national levels. In this way, as they struggle to ensure the survival of their culture, indigenous people also have contributed to the democratization of the educational system by promoting the participation of local communities in choosing their teachers, who are important political actors in the countryside.

The story of bilingual intercultural education in Ecuador demonstrates that the indigenous movement, by organizing to defend its culture, is affecting the political system. This trend can be further demonstrated by examining the issue of agrarian production in the modernization program of President Durán.

AGRARIAN DEVELOPMENT AND THE INDIGENOUS VOICE

State-led economic reforms are providing the impetus for protests throughout the Americas. Many observers of Latin American politics have noted that the shift from developmentalist to neoliberal economic models is accompanied by structural adjustment policies that have a strong impact on the poorer sectors of society. The indigenous movement is providing a political voice for one of the most excluded sectors of Ecuadoran society — the part of the population that considers itself indigenous. By questioning the economic issues that affect its people, such as land tenure, the indigenous movement challenges new policies for liberal economic reform in the country.[51]

This section will demonstrate how, by demanding participation for the indigenous sector, leaders of the movement are challenging the lack of democratic participation in the national political system. Within that context, by defining itself as a social group excluded from the country's economic and political development, the indigenous movement may provide the opportunity to disclose structural inequalities in the political system and to propose alternatives.

Today in Ecuador, as in much of Latin America, politics is largely defined by government-led economic reforms focused on the privatization of national industries, liberalization of market restrictions, and technological advancement in industry, particularly in the export sector. As many analysts have noted, these reforms tend to affect the poorer sectors of society dramatically, whose members previously benefited from job security or price controls. The impact on the lower classes has led to social unrest in many cases. In Ecuador, the reforms were implemented through President Durán's 1994 "Modernization Law."

One of the most important economic sectors affected by privatization also directly impacts indigenous subsistence economy; that sector is small-scale agricultural production in the Highlands. As Ecuador is predominantly an agrarian society, a priority for further development of the country is the modernization of the agricultural sector. While production of sugarcane and bananas for export is mechanized in the coastal region, the majority of agricultural production in the Highlands is traditional crop production for national consumption. Plans for modernizing the agricultural sector, in the form of the Modernization Law, provoked controversy and social unrest, as once again the indigenous sector demanded to be included in the formulation of those plans. When the law was eventually passed, it contained substantive changes negotiated with the indigenous sector, as will be described in the following section.

The Ecuadoran Institute of Agrarian Reform and Colonization (IERAC) has regulated rural land tenure in Ecuador since its creation by the 1964 Agrarian Reform Law. The military government (1963-1966) decreed this law as part of the first large-scale attempt to abolish the semifeudal agrarian system and address the unequal distribution of land in the countryside. The law's main effect was the transformation of the poor, mostly indigenous rural population from indentured servants into rural laborers. Nearly a decade later, General Guillermo Rodríguez Lara, the populist military ruler,

Indigenous leaders with Luis Macas during 1994 Agrarian Reform protests

implemented a second Agrarian Reform Law in 1973 in an attempt to strengthen the agrarian reform process. Article 30 of that law provided for the expropriation of lands that were not sufficiently productive; this part of the 1973 Agrarian Reform Law established a basis for indigenous takeovers (land recuperation) of large landholdings.[52]

The general goal of Ecuador's original agrarian reform laws, which resembled those of other countries in the region, was the redistribution of land and the abolition of semifeudal agricultural practices, to promote small independent farms and modern capitalist relations in the countryside. In the 1980s and 1990s, new agrarian reform proposals emerged that corresponded with the neoliberal economic model, which continues to influence development policies throughout Latin America. This more recent agrarian project promotes modernization of agricultural practices in general and the agricultural export industry in particular. The indigenous movement is struggling against these reforms in Ecuador in order to defend certain legal protections provided them in the original agrarian reform laws.

The indigenous response to agrarian modernization plans took shape when President Durán presented a proposal to Congress in 1993 for an Agrarian Development Law. His proposed law favored agribusiness and the elimination of government intervention in the agricultural market. This proposal fit Durán's policy of privatization, in that it sought to modernize the country and quell inflation by increasing free market influences on the economy. However, CONAIE immediately protested the proposal, arguing that it represented the interests of only a small sector of society and represented an attack on the lifestyle of the rural, indigenous population.[53]

Changes in land-tenure policy are of great concern to indigenous groups. Ecuador's Constitution acknowledges four types of land holdings: private, public, mixed, and communal. Durán's proposed Agrarian Development Law, CONAIE feared, would recognize only private property, disavowing the communal land ownership important to many indigenous communities. CONAIE declared the proposal unconstitutional and took an unexpected step: It united with other rural organizations, including some historic adversaries such as FENOC-I, to form the National Agrarian Coordinator and develop an alternative agrarian law proposal.

The National Agrarian Coordinator, guided by CONAIE's legal advisors, carried out the actual investigation and elaboration of the alternative agrarian law. The alternative law was developed through a series of consultations, congresses, and workshops so that it would represent not just the ideas of CONAIE's intellectuals, but also those of indigenous people and campesinos throughout the county.

The alternative law proposed by the rural organizations focused on three principal issues: 1) production for internal consumption instead of export, 2) participation in decisionmaking at various levels of the political system, and 3) fair distribution of land. Moreover, it called for respect for communal landholding traditions, preservation of indigenous territories, and protection of the environment. The proposal suggested that to increase production, small farmers would need to receive government incentives such as financial credits, rather than invest all their small plots in agribusiness.[54]

On June 9, 1993, the National Agrarian Coordinator led a peaceful march of hundreds indigenous leaders and their supporters to the Congress to present their alternative proposal. The President of Congress, Carlos Vallejo, refused to receive the National Agrarian Coordinator's appointed delegation. Instead, he called upon heavily armed police to guard the Congress building. The event became violent, and the marchers were tear-gassed and beaten with billy clubs.

The news coverage of the march and its violent reception, showing Luís Macas, CONAIE's president, being beaten over the head by police in front of the National Congress was in shocking contrast to the previous administration's respectful treatment of CONAIE's representatives. In response to the repression and to further protest the privatization plans being debated in Congress, the National Agrarian Coordinator called for a second protest to begin the following week, on June 15, 1993.

The short-lived uprising of June 1993 resulted in the closing of part of the Pan-American Highway for a few days. The protests coincided, however, with soccer World Cup events that were being hosted by Ecuador that year. The indigenous leadership hoped to take advantage of the presence of international media to show the world that "while they play the America's Cup [soccer]... they also are playing with the poverty and misery of Ecuadorans."[55] The government and the national media in general accused the indigenous organizers of attempting to undermine the World Cup and promote a negative image of Ecuador, a country touted as an "island of peace" in the Andes and a haven for tourism. The unrest was stabilized quickly, and the government's agrarian law proposal was temporarily shelved.

Although the 1993 agrarian law protests were short-lived, they brought the debate about agrarian law forcefully into the public sphere. Discussion of the law was postponed as members of Congress and the public questioned its validity. The Agrarian Coordinator submitted its alternative proposal to Congress to be studied and debated. This proposal, in fact, was never introduced to the floor for debate; instead, it was filed with the Agriculture Committee of Congress.

One year later, without official discussions of the topic between government and indigenous groups, the 1994 Agrarian Development Law was presented to Congress by the Social Christian Party, was passed, and was signed into law by President Durán on June 13, 1994. This law held to the same basic principles as Durán's proposed 1993 law, with marginal language added to address indigenous and ecological issues.

Indigenous organizations said that the 1994 Agrarian Development Law was geared toward developing the agricultural export industry at the cost of small farmers, the same objection they had raised regarding the president's proposed 1993 agrarian development law. Article 15 of the 1994 law, for example, gave a five-year, 50-percent tax break to new agro-industry businesses. The bias toward agro-industry in the law, indigenous groups asserted, directly challenged indigenous people's rights to small farms, credits, and even their communal way of life. "The indigenous people cannot accept a law that promotes the re-concentration of land in the same hands as always and that prohibits indigenous communities' access to land so that we, with no place to grow, will have to leave to die of hunger and misery in the cities."[56]

In the Amazon, indigenous groups feared that the new law would promote colonization of the rain forest. Although the law mentioned ecological protection as a secondary point in some articles, the groups felt that it was not adequately elaborated or inclusive of monitoring measures. In Article 36, for example, after describing how the new law will help ethnic groups in the Amazon incorporate new technology, a policy that is questioned by CONAIE, the text states, "The actions, methods, and instruments used should preserve the ecological system."[57] In the Amazon, as in the

Highlands, the general observation of indigenous groups was that the agrarian reform law of the past had been replaced without their input.

The indigenous communities demanded that the law be overturned on the basis of its unconstitutionality, as the new law had been passed without the 15 days of debate required by Article 65 of the Constitution. The indigenous organizations had repeatedly called for national debate concerning agrarian reform. Now they complained that the government was attempting to bypass that debate by putting the law through so quickly.

To protest Durán's Agrarian Development Law, on June 14, 1994, the indigenous organizations united, and the National Agrarian Coordinator again staged a national uprising. This time, hundreds of thousands of indigenous protestors closed strategic points along the Pan-American Highway, preventing transportation of agricultural products to the cities and refusing to bring their own produce to market. In some towns, government buildings were taken over, and up to 30,000 people at a time filled city streets in marches throughout the country. In the Amazon, along with setting up effective roadblocks, indigenous communities took over three oil wells, and oil production was halted for days.

On June 22, 1994, President Durán announced a "mobilization decree," giving the armed forces free rein to do whatever was necessary to halt the protests.[58] On June 23, the Tribunal of Constitutional Guarantees officially upheld the indigenous organizations' petition that the law was unconstitutional and sent the case to the Supreme Court. The president declared the pronouncement of the tribunal invalid but agreed to meet with the indigenous leadership to try to resolve the dispute.

As a result of the dialogue between the indigenous leadership and President Durán, a commission was formed that included disparate members of society who were affected by the law. Participants in the commission included indigenous and campesino representatives; members of the Dairy Farmers Association, a historically conservative and anti-indigenous group; members of government ministries; and the president. The main topics of discussion were water rights, land tenancy, and agricultural credits. The indigenous representatives came to the first meeting of the commission with video cameras, indigenous lawyers, and technical points for analysis. The CONAIE media team was present to ensure adequate coverage of the dialogue for the public, especially for the indigenous communities. "You should have seen their faces! They never expected us to come so prepared," one participant recalled.[59] *After weeks of debate, the working commission unanimously approved notable changes in the Agrarian Development Law of 1994, which included many of the indigenous people's demands.*

The events surrounding the Agrarian Development Law demonstrate how the indigenous movement is publicly challenging the exclusion of civil society from political decisionmaking in Ecuador. At the same time, CONAIE is providing a vehicle for sectors of civil society to present their interests to the government. If CONAIE did not exist, perhaps the original agrarian law might have passed with little concern among the small rural landholders directly affected by it, since they are generally ill-informed about developments in government. CONAIE's effort to intervene directly in the system, by proposing an alternative law to Congress and petitioning the Tribunal of Constitutional Guarantees, was not effective. United by a mass demonstration of strength through protests, however, CONAIE was able to bring its position to the negotiating table at the presidential level. CONAIE clearly stated that not only landholdings were at stake — also at stake was the very survival of indigenous cultures, which are centered on land relations and the cycles of agricultural production.

INDIGENOUS RIGHTS AND DEMOCRATIZATION

The case of the indigenous response to modernization of the agrarian sector and the case of the struggle for bilingual education both illustrate the thesis of this book. By demanding participation in the political process concerning issues that affect them, indigenous leaders are challenging the lack of democratic participation in the system as a whole. To compare the two situations, one can consider the following questions: How does the indigenous movement affect the distribution of power and the structures of the political system? And is identity an effective way for civil society to organize?

In regard to the distribution of power, both cases suggest that the indigenous movement, while mobilizing around sectarian issues, did indeed affect political institutions. The creation of a bilingual education system not only challenged the hegemony of Hispanic culture, as described above; it also broke the practice by which political party representatives named teachers in return for political favors such as money and votes. Beyond undermining clientelistic relations, the indigenous movement was able to institutionalize indigenous participation in the Ministry of Education and Culture through the creation of the Directorate of Bilingual Intercultural Education (DINEIB).

The agrarian law battle did not lead to the institutionalization of indigenous participation in the Ministry of Agriculture. However, it did create a forum for participation in the specific issue of agrarian law: a presidential commission, through which indigenous groups were able to alter the law significantly in their favor. Moreover, the movement challenged the unofficial authority of the "unholy alliance" of capitalist agricultural producers and the urban elite, mostly traders — an alliance that traditionally has controlled power and economic relations in rural Ecuador.[60] The large agricultural producers, particularly the Association of Dairy Farmers, were contributing authors of the original Agrarian Development Law. By protesting the law, the indigenous sector challenged the authority of the producers and the elite to define agricultural policy for the entire country. This was an issue of democratic participation, in which the indigenous sector demanded participation in defining policies that would affect it.

The second question refers to the effectiveness of political organizing based on identity, specifically ethnic identification. Again, both cases in this chapter confirm the effectiveness of identity-based organizing, particularly in a context of exclusion. Indigenous communities have been excluded from direct economic and political power in Ecuador; thus they question their very citizenship in the nation, as described above. As indigenous peoples, then, their basic complaint against the Ecuadoran state is that they should be included; in other words, they should be given the opportunity to participate in the government. Exclusion, however, has allowed for the continued existence of a separate identity that unites indigenous communities as an organizational sector and unites them in the desire for some sort of participation. Inherently, I contend, their political demands are centered on democratic participation.

The struggle for participation in the educational system finally was considered legitimate because the movement represented a large sector of society that sought to strengthen its identity. An indirect result of this participation was the political opening within the education system. The agrarian struggle, while intrinsically a material question of land rights, appeared to have more legitimacy because of the link between indigenous culture and the land; the identity factor gave it unity. The underlying call for inclusion resulted in strong mobilizations in support of indigenous land rights.

Conclusion

This chapter aimed to bring to light some political ramifications of the discussions about social movements in Latin America. Identity-based movements, although organized around the interests of a specific sector, can successfully lead to broader democratic openings in the system as a whole. Because they often are developed in response to a context of exclusion from economic and political power, identity-based movements usually are centered around demands for access to power or political participation. Political participation, as many theorists have suggested, is central to democratic reform.

In the case of Ecuador, as this chapter has demonstrated, the indigenous population has largely been excluded since the Spanish conquest; however, despite attempts at mass acculturation, a large percentage of the rural population has maintained a distinct identity. Contemporary circumstances have led to the development of a unique indigenous ideology that forms the essence of the contemporary indigenous movement. That movement, with CONAIE at the forefront, has spread a new concept of indigenous identity. Beyond the development of an ideology, the indigenous movement has made concrete changes in the political system, as exemplified in the two cases described here: bilingual education and agrarian reform. The bilingual education program changed the nature of politics in the countryside by wresting power from the traditional ruling elite. The agrarian reform protests enshrined indigenous access rights in the country's agrarian law.

Notes

1. Santiago Nieto, 1993, "El problema indígena," in *Los indios y el Estado-País*, ed. Diego Cornejo Menacho (Quito: Abya-Yala), 61.

2. A political representative in Loja province interviewed by author in 1993.

3. Paola Sylva Charvet, 1991, *La organización rural en el Ecuador* (Quito: Abya-Yala).

4. See Corporación de Estudios y Publicaciones; Updated in 1993, *Ley de Colonización de la Región Amazónica*, 89.

5. See Corporación de Estudios y Publicaciones; Updated in 1993, *Ley de Tierras Baldías y Colonización*, 99.

6. Apam Karakras, 1991, Shuar, director of finances for CONAIE, interview by author.

7. A leader from Bolívar province, 1991, interview by author.

8. Manuel Medina, 1993, CIOIS (Coordinadora Interprovincial de Organizaciones Indígenas), interview by author.

9. In 1994, overall illiteracy in the country was 10 percent, and it was four times higher in the countryside (17.4 percent) than in the city (4.9 percent). See Agustín Grijalva, 1994, Datos Básicos de la Realidad Nacional (Quito: Corporación Editora Nacional).

10. This definition is borrowed from Raymond Geuss, 1981, The Idea of Critical Theory: Habermas and the Frankfurt School (New York: Cambridge University Press). For a discussion of about ideology, see Terry Eagleton, 1991, *Ideology: An Introduction* (New York: Verso Books). Modern discussion of ideology considers that the subordinate classes can develop an ideology that can challenge that of the dominant classes. Thus, ideology is linked to social transformation.

11. Ernesto Laclau and Chantal Mouffe, for example. See their 1985 volume, *Hegemony and Socialist Strategy: Towards a Radical Democratic Politics* (London: Verso).

12. María Paca, 1993, Bilingual Education Project, CONAIE, interview by author.

13. Eckstein 1989, 23.

14. Macas, 1993, interview by author.

15. Alicia Ibarra, ed., 1987, *Los indígenas y el Estado en el Ecuador* (Quito: Abya-Yala). "Dominant culture" is an anthropological concept referring to the cultural group that controls the sources of hegemony in a society.

16. Based on the author's interviews with indigenous leaders.

17. Frank, Patiño, and Rodríguez 1992, 71.

18. Zamosc 1994, 282.

19. However, some current indigenous leaders were involved in an armed movement in Colombia in the past. Also, some past members of the Ecuadoran subversive organization,

Alfaro Vive, Carajo, who at the time were critical of the movement, now are working closely with indigenous issues.

20. See Enrique Ayala Mora, 1989, *Los partidos políticos en el Ecuador* (Quito: Ediciones la Tierra) for general description of parties in Ecuador.

21. Lluco, 1991, interview by author.

22. Karakras, 1991, interview by author.

23. Identity is referred to in this context as collective identity not as personal identity. The question of personal identity is too complex to elaborate upon in this discussion, although it is definitely important. Here, I refer to group political identity.

24. See Crain 1990, for a wonderful discussion of indigenous counter-hegemony in the Highlands province of Ecuador.

25. Karakras, 1991, interview by author.

26. See Belote and Belote 1984, for detailed discussion of this phenomenon in Saraguro, Ecuador.

27. Miguel Ángel Carlosamán, 1991, FICI (Indigenous Federation of Imbabura), interview by author.

28. León 1994, 51.

29. For a summary of CONAIE demands, see Appendix 4: COAIE Demands to the Government, 1990 Uprising: The Pluri-National Mandate.

30. The National Agrarian Development Institute (INDA) replaced the Ecuadoran Institute for Agrarian Reform and Colonization (IERAC) in 1994.

31. A fascinating tale of political debate about the "pluri-national state" can be found in Robert Andolina's unpublished 1998 paper "CONAIE (and Others) in the Ambiguous Spaces of Democracy: Positioning for the 1997-1998 Asemblea Nacional Constituyente in Ecuador" (Latin American Studies Association — LASA).

32. CONAIE, 1994, El Estado Plurinacional (Quito: Impreso CONAIE), 52.

33. Osvaldo Hurtado, 1993, Gobernabilidad y reforma constitutional (Quito: Corporación Editora Nacional), 33.

34. Macas 1991, 132.

35. Andrango, 1991, interview by author.

36. José Quimbo, 1993, Indigenous Affairs Office of President Sixto Durán Ballén, interview by author.

37. ECUARUNARI, ed., 1989, *Nuestra voz, Nuestra cultura: Taller Andino de Intercambio de Experiencias en Educación y Comunicación de Organizaciones Campesino-Indígenas* (Quito: ECUARUNARI), 95.

38. Samuel Ortega, 1993, FIIS (Inter-provincial Federation of Indigenous Saraguros), interview by author.

39. Consuelo Yánez Cossío, 1991, *"Macac": Teoría y práctica de la educación indígena — Estudio de caso en el Ecuador* (Cali, Colombia: CELATER — Centro Latinoamericano de Tecnología y Educación Rural), 97.

40. Muenala, 1993, interview by author.

41. Grijalva 1994, 125.

42. Tránsito Chela, 1993, Directorate of Bilingual Intercultural Education, interview by author.

43. Yánez, 1991, 88.

44. Based on the author's interviews with participants.

45. Monteluisa, 1993, interview by author.

46. Monteluisa, 1993, interview by author.

47. Calderón, 1993, interview by author.

48. Observations based on the author's field research and informational interviews.

49. Zamosc 1994, 8-9.

50. See "Indígenas Aclaran Situación de Educación Bilingüe," press release, December 23, 1992, CONAIE archives.

51. Deborah Yashar links the shift from campesino to indigenous identity (as a basis for collective action) to changes in economic policy. See Yashar 1999.

52. The indigenous groups call these takeovers "land recuperation," while the dominant Spanish society refers to them as "land invasions." This is an interesting comment on discourse when one considers use of the term "invasion" by Indians to describe the Spanish conquest.

53. Durán's agrarian development law was fueled by the agricultural sector loan of the Inter-American Development Bank's (IDB). For a fascinating analysis of the role of the multilateral development banks and international support networks with the indigenous movement in Ecuador, see Kay Treakle, 1998, "Ecuador: Structural Adjustment and Indigenous and Environmental Resistance," in *The Struggle for Accountability: The World Bank, NGOs, and Grassroots Movements*, eds. Jonathan Fox and L. David Brown (Cambridge, Mass.: MIT Press), 219-264.

54. "Internal Agrarian Reform Project" (alternative agrarian law proposal), published by CONAIE for the public.

55. Luis Macas, quoted in Voz de la CONFENIAE (newsletter), June 1993, 2.

56. CONAIE press release, June 14, 1994.

57. CONAIE press release, June 14, 1994.

58. The "mobilization decree" stopped short of a state of emergency. It called for military mobilization without stricter measures, such as control of the press.

59. These statements were obtained from the author's interview with a member of the CONAIE team, 1994.

60. The term "unholy alliance" originally referred to the alliance between hacienda owners and the Catholic Church. That alliance was replaced by the modern one with the growth of capitalism and agrarian reform. See Tanya Karovkin,1993, *Indians, Peasants, and the State: The Growth of a Community Movement in the Ecuadoran Andes*, Occasional Paper No. 3 (Ontario: Center for Research on Latin America and the Caribbean — York University), 12.

Chapter 6

Local Indigenous Politics: Three Cases in Rural Ecuador

INTRODUCTION

Scholars of political processes in Latin America increasingly are observing the need for systems of political participation to be established in the rural sector.[1] While free and fair elections are an important indicator of democracy, citizenship rights encompass more than participation in elections. It is important, then, to consider the extent to which those other political rights are practiced. According to Jonathan Fox, "The rights of political citizenship in a democracy include guaranteed basic civil and political freedoms, majority rule with minority rights, the equitable administration of justice, as well as respect for associational autonomy."[2]

Chapter 5 described a case in which the indigenous movement challenged entrenched clientelistic practices by taking control of the education of indigenous communities. The movement undermined politicians' influence in the countryside by taking control of the educational system from them, particularly through winning the right to name teachers in the indigenous-populated rural areas. In rural Ecuador, that is, among the population outside the country's two

Amazonian Quichua at 1994 Agrarian Protests

largest cities, Quito and Guayaquil, indigenous communities now use their newly identified political voice to challenge existing practices. Their demands, coming from an excluded sector of society, naturally include increased representation and participation in decision-making structures.

Analytical discussions within Ecuador about the rise of the indigenous movement focus on the material causes for the recent surge in indigenous activism. The general argument is that the fall in market prices for agricultural goods, the growth of land monopolies, and the lack of land to relieve population pressures all contributed to an economic depression in the countryside that caused the poor to protest.[3] Material need is an important mobilizing factor, as much of the literature on social movements demonstrates, but an ideological context is also necessary for groups to organize as a movement. To portray the indigenous movement as an unorganized popular tide rising up against the forces of capital is inaccurate. An entrenched ideological perspective now pervades indigenous communities throughout the country and unites them despite their diverse circumstances. Indeed, material conditions were quite disparate in the three provinces I studied, suggesting that the ideological awareness of indigenous identity and rights provided the framework for a unified movement.

This chapter will examine the relations between the indigenous movement and local government in three provinces: Bolívar and Loja, both Andean regions; and an Amazonian province, Pastaza. Despite diverse socioeconomic conditions, each province boasts a vociferous and well-organized local indigenous movement. My field research in the provinces became an exploration of the ideology of the indigenous movement: How do indigenous people perceive themselves and their relationship to the government and to the nation? How are they viewed by local society and government? After a brief description of rural political structures in Ecuador in general, the three cases will be compared. For each case, this chapter provides general background information, a description of the growth of indigenous organization, and examples of traditional clientelism and new forms of indigenous political participation.

RURAL POLITICAL STRUCTURE

As pointed out in Chapter 2, Ecuador is an "unfinished nation," a fact that is relevant for understanding the recent success of the indigenous movement. This chapter will build on that premise by demonstrating that although Ecuador enjoys relative stability compared to its neighbors, its *democracy* is also unfinished. As is common in agrarian societies, democratic institutions that function reasonably well in the city are not equally available or functional in the countryside, both in terms of institutions and citizenship.

The clientelism that dominates rural political decisions can restrict the basic freedoms necessary for citizenship, as Fox points out in the case of Mexico.[4] As in Mexico, in Ecuador it is common for a rural community to promise votes to a politician in exchange for basic needs (such as potable water, a school, a road, or a bridge). Requests for these needs are made to the elected official, rather than to a neutral administrative office. This kind of negotiation of goods and services for votes is a common form of clientelism. According to local indigenous communities, the unfair distribution of a province's developmental resources is exacerbated by the racism against indigenous peoples that pervades government institutions. Numerous indigenous informants testified to being turned away at government offices or waiting all day while mestizo visitors passed ahead of them: "The one with the poncho was always left to wait while the one wearing a tie went ahead."[5] Many indigenous communities believe that local government institutions represent not them, but rather a foreign, mestizo society, even at the local level.

Since its inception, a central demand of the indigenous movement in Ecuador has been citizenship. While local demands might appear to focus on material needs, participating in the national indigenous movement and sharing its ideology puts indigenous communities in a position to demand equal treatment as citizens of Ecuador and to win acknowledgment of their right to citizenship without sacrificing their identity.

Political control in the countryside continues to perpetuate the power base inherited by the landed elites. The structure includes an elected municipal council, an elected prefect for the province, a governor representing the president of the republic, and "political lieutenants," who are appointed by the governor for each canton. A canton is the political division around each town in a province. Mestizos, even in the predominantly indigenous areas such as Bolívar, fill virtually all the positions.[6] In a few instances, one finds indigenous deputies and lieutenants. I will refer to all these representatives of local government as the "local authorities."

The governor names local authorities according to political allegiances and promises made during electoral campaigns. Before DINEIB, the bilingual education directorate, teachers were named in the same fashion. In choosing the individuals to fill vacant posts, technical qualifications are much less important than political affiliations.[7]

Table 1 (below), based on the national census of 1990, shows the percentage of indigenous (Indian) inhabitants of three of Ecuador's 22 provinces and the total percentage for the entire country. The census is widely recognized as an extremely conservative estimate, but it does present a useful ratio for comparison. In other words, it demonstrates that the indigenous population is much smaller in Loja than in the other two provinces. CONAIE rejects these percentages entirely, based on the fact that the census was carried out by mestizos, to whom indigenous individuals may have wanted to mask their indigenous identity. The table also shows, in the second column, whether each province has an Office for Indian Affairs, including the federal government.

Table 1. Indigenous Population by Province, 1993

	% Indian	Indian Affairs Staff
Bolívar	21	yes
Loja/Saraguro	3	no
Pastaza	29	yes
Ecuador (total)	16	yes

Source: Government of Ecuador, 1990, *National Census*.[8]

BOLÍVAR

Background

B olívar is a typical province of the Ecuadoran Highlands in many respects. Fundamentally agricultural and politically and economically isolated by a ring of seven volcanoes, Bolívar has a large indigenous population, extremely unequal division of wealth, and a vigorous political patronage system. The indigenous federation in Bolívar is a canny participant in the clientelistic politics of the province, regularly endorsing candidates in exchange for favors in its community. The politicians, in turn, recognize the importance of indigenous support and cater to the community in their public policies or at least in their pronouncements.

The province of Bolívar is made up of *minifundias*, or small farms, with a few larger associations or cooperatives and very little mechanized production. Professionals, including indigenous professionals, tend to move to Quito or other nearby cities but not to the small provincial capital of Guaranda, resulting in an endemic brain drain.

Resolution of land conflicts, securing potable water, getting fair prices for products, and solving local infrastructure problems are high on the list of indigenous priorities in Bolívar. In addition, ethnic pride pervades all the discourse in this province. For example, according to the leaders of the Bolívar indigenous federation, "We, too, are capable of demanding our rights, even though the mestizos of Bolívar thought the indigenous were incapable."[9] One example of creative protest tactics used by the indigenous organizations in Bolívar is as follows: On October 12, 1992, the quincentennial of the arrival of Columbus in the New World, a massive indigenous march was held at which local authorities were presented a symbolic "bill" for their broken promises to the indigenous community.

Provincial Indigenous Federation

The Bolívar Campesino Federation (Federación Campesina de Bolívar — FECAB) was founded in 1972 by five communities. By 1991, some 80 communities had joined, with others waiting to become affiliates at the next Congress of the federation.[10] Why the dramatic increase? It is clear that 1) the organization has been partially successful in directing resources to indigenous communities, 2) the process of bilingual education has promoted contemporary indigenous ideology in the region, and 3) the organization has become an interlocutor of development and other projects for indigenous communities. In other words, now that the federation speaks on behalf of indigenous communities, the communities want a vote. The federation has gained enough recognition in the province that even mestizo communities have asked to join and have been accepted as members.

Bolívar provides an example of the influence of bilingual literacy programs on the indigenous movement, as discussed in Chapter 5. In the 1970s, the leadership of FECAB, along with the Provincial Department of

Bilingual bi-cultural education students in Bolívar province

Indian Affairs, took part in adult literacy campaigns that took them to most of the Quichua-speaking communities in the province. They credit this relationship with the communities for their election to their respective positions.[11]

The indigenous movement of Bolívar has consistently demanded that the local government fulfill its campaign promises. For example, Freddy Espinoza, the mayor of Guaranda, in 1991 represented a party on the left that campaigned with the slogan: "The land should belong to those who work it." FECAB leaders met with him regularly thereafter, demanding his intervention in land disputes.

Local Government

The perspective of the mestizo in Bolívar can be considered representative of the entire country. Since the 1990 Uprising, Quichua language and dress have found increasing acceptance. Yet, a tangible division remains between the "city" and the "country" along racial lines. Local politicians try to obscure this division along ethnic lines, proposing that "there is only one population; the people from the city and the people from the countryside are all Ecuadoran. . . . We are all mestizos."[12] Statements like this reject the indigenous organizations' platform, which calls for equal, yet different, recognition of citizenship.

Bolívar's local authorities are from land-owning families, often related to the feudal families that dominated through the early part of the century. In general, they are ethnically more Spanish than mestizo. When the provincial authorities in Bolívar do support the indigenous communities, they benefit from the relationship in a number of ways. First and foremost, they count on their votes. All officials I interviewed credited their election victories to the indigenous vote. Many of them used the indigenous vote repeatedly as a source of legitimacy. For example, the prefect Roberto Llerena, elected in August 1992, stated, "My presence here in the council is basically due to the support of the indigenous people, as a consequence of the responsible work I have demonstrated toward them."[13]

The local authorities in Bolívar take advantage of free indigenous labor in the form of volunteer communal work parties (called *mingas*) to stretch their limited infrastructure's budgets. When a community approaches the provincial council and requests a bridge, for example, the authority is likely to offer to supply the materials and a government technician if the community will supply the manual labor. It is a long-standing tradition for indigenous community members to call a *minga* for projects that benefit the whole community, and the authorities realize they can take advantage of this. The indigenous organizations expressed pride in this custom and in their willingness to contribute to the development of their communities. At the same time, they questioned the justice of the national government spending more money in urban areas, where authorities do not have the benefit of the *minga* to exploit.

Military

Indigenous organizations in Bolívar appeared to have a fraternal relationship with the local military brigade during the period of this study. Regular, good-natured meetings took place between FECAB and the military. FECAB often received support, in the form of food and shelter, from the military brigade for its general assemblies.

Clientelism/Citizenship

The current office of FECAB, a new two-story building in the center of town, was paid for by the Democratic Left Party (ID) in exchange for the political support of the indigenous communities in elections. In addition, indigenous groups formed a united front in support of the ID for the 1992 elections in exchange for a seat for an indigenous representative on the provincial council. Because the indigenous leader was given only the position of alternate councilman, FECAB considered itself betrayed by the party. The party did come through on its commitment to open a Ministry of Indigenous Affairs, headed by an indigenous leader who participates in the provincial meetings of the Council of Ministers. Another important electoral promise was the construction of the FECAB offices, which local authorities also promised to furnish.

When the new FECAB offices were opened, a huge housewarming party (in Quichua, a *huasifichay* or housecleaning) was given in accordance with an indigenous tradition that has become an Ecuadoran custom. This event took place in July 1993, approximately one year after the new officials took office. Local officials were invited, and many of them, especially those with a public commitment to indigenous people, were in attendance. The prefect was invited to sit on a chair upstairs, on a balcony overlooking the courtyard, and to give a little speech. All of a sudden, the prefect's chair was pulled into the air by a rope, and he was literally left hanging above the crowds. "Mr. Prefect," called the laughing leaders, "what will you give us to let you down?" The prefect, literally hanging from a rope two stories above his jovial indigenous constituents, was obliged to repeat his preelection promises to the organization. One by one, the local government authorities were "hung." By the end of the evening, in front of several hundred indigenous community members, they had promised to finish the construction of the FECAB offices and to furnish them completely.

Clientelism is basically political bargaining, but it can be differentiated from more democratic political bargaining by analyzing the balance of power and political rights. Fox discusses the relations of domination that can prevent the pursuit of democratic freedoms. Those who are dominated exercise and sacrifice their bargaining power in exchange for basic goods and services.[14] FECAB is now taking back its bargaining power. The indigenous organizations in Bolívar inherited a political system in which indigenous communities had lived in a debt-peonage system for hundreds of years. The political culture of clientelism is still strong. Yet, in demanding that the politicians keep their promises and by doing so through their traditional expressions of communal power (symbolized by the housewarming and the "hanging"), the indigenous movement is clearly taking important steps toward gaining full citizenship rights.

Another example of the shift toward citizenship can be seen in the education system. The impact of the bilingual education program on clientelism at the national level was discussed in Chapter 5. In Bolívar, the switch to indigenous teachers appears to have had a dramatic impact. Until recently, indigenous parents had to give gifts to the mestizo teachers who came from town to assure that their children would be taught, according to interviews. "The indigenous parents had to bring eggs, cheese, milk, or a small chicken to the teacher. Why? So he would teach their children!"[15] While many problems still plague the bilingual education system, the indigenous communities with whom I met spoke very clearly of their right to a school and education for their children.

Pastaza

Background

Pastaza is an important Amazon province that is a gateway to the tropical rain forest and home to both indigenous communities and mestizo settlers who have immigrated from other parts of the country. Most of the region's production is based on family subsistence, with some fruit production and dairy farming by settler families.

In general, land conflicts in the Amazon are of a different nature than those of the Highlands. They usually consist of either disputes between indigenous peoples and settlers or an indigenous community's claim for title to prevent further colonization of their ancestral territory, which, according to international law, includes hunting and gathering lands, not just the village.[16] The two largest ethnic groups in the Amazon, the lowland Quichua and the Huaorani, were granted substantial collective land titles during the Borja administration (1988-1992). The collective Quichua territory is in Pastaza, and the Organization of Indigenous Peoples of Pastaza (Organización de Pueblos Indígenas de Pastaza — OPIP) holds the title.

The Amazon has a less mixed population than the other areas of Ecuador because colonization by mestizos has been more recent. Identity is

Communities in Pastaza are fighting to protect their rainforest home.

less fluid, and cultural differences are greater between indigenous and other communities. Tensions can run high, particularly over land disputes and environmental protection issues, to the extent that the governor of Pastaza stated in an interview that his main responsibility was to "keep the peace among the different communities."[17]

Provincial Indigenous Organization

The OPIP has become a political force in the province. Since its foundation in 1979 by three communities (Sarayacu, Arajuno, and San Jacinto), it has come to include most of the Quichua communities in the province. It has a strong affiliation with the national organization, CONAIE. (Some Amazonian organizations have political conflicts with CONAIE, claiming that it represents only the views of the Highlands indigenous communities). OPIP gained global attention when its members marched to the capital to demand their ancestral territory, which subsequently was given to them in the form of a communal land title in 1991.

OPIP was formed specifically to counteract the dramatic problem of settlers' invasions of indigenous territories and the resulting conflicts, which often were violent. Racism against indigenous people was pervasive, organizers say, and their leaders suffered persecution as a result. "Nobody understood us or wanted anything to do with us at that time. The settler [mestizo] society humiliated us, so very few communities came forward to join us," stated OPIP founder Hector Villamil.[18]

Since most conflicts over land ownership between settlers and indigenous communities were resolved during the Borja administration, the organization now is focused primarily on education, health and development programs, and resolution of conflicts about oil production.

Regarding oil production, two main points cause concern. First, oil development directly damages the environment and, thus, the cultural integrity of the indigenous communities of the Amazon. Oil production always brings new roads and an influx of settlers competing for fertile land. Historically, oil companies bring in their own labor supply, which includes families that usually remain in the region. Exploration for oil, drilling and pipeline construction, and maintenance lead to countless environmental tragedies, including spillage of crude oil and toxic wastes, contamination of water, and destruction of plant and animal species. Other Amazon provinces with oil activities have witnessed the rapid disappearance of indigenous cultures because of disease and habitat destruction.[19] Given the evidence of those experiences, the indigenous organization in Pastaza is concerned for the very survival of the communities it represents.

A second concern is the divisions within the indigenous movement caused by the entrance of oil companies. While the indigenous organizations are concerned with the environment of the Amazon as a whole, the individual communities often are concerned with their own welfare, including their desire for the kind of material goods that oil companies offer as incentives for agreement to their entrance into an indigenous territory. These incentives range from corrugated tin for roofing to school buildings. The village of Villano in Pastaza provides an example of the internal conflicts oil development can cause. ARCO, an international oil company, was digging a well there, and some families accepted ARCO's presence by accepting its gifts as well as employment with the company. Others, with the support of OPIP, rejected oil drilling in their environment.

The conflict in Villano presents a microcosm of the contradictions inherent in nationalist development models and democratic pluralism, as discussed in Chapter 2. As indigenous communities have been excluded from the political system, they have been unable to influence development concerns in their regions. In the Amazon, an extreme case, entire indigenous nationalities have been annihilated in the name of development. Their perspective was not included in political debates, nor did they have a voice until recent decades. Now, they are struggling to define their voice in a context of inequality and confusion. In many cases, a community leader must ally with a specific political party to get basic necessities for the community. For such a leader to keep the respect of the community, he or she must come through by fulfilling the people's material needs. In Pastaza, the indigenous people have two other options: For a political voice, they can rely on the strength of OPIP, and for development projects, they can turn to the oil company. Unfortunately, these choices contradict each other.

OPIP is attempting to attend to the development needs of communities in the province by negotiating with the military, the central government, and the local government. While these institutions do cooperate, they usually prefer to negotiate directly with communities to promote new leadership. One of the chronic criticisms of indigenous organizations is that they tend to reelect the same leaders, and relatively few new leaders seem to emerge. Héctor Villamil, for example, has been in the leadership of OPIP since it was founded, and he has held the office of president four times. Such continuity of leadership should be noted as a characteristic of the organizations.

A smaller organization in Pastaza called the Colonist Federation of Pastaza (Federación de Colonos de Pastaza — FEDECAP) does similar work for local communities, but it does not organize on the basis of identity. On the contrary, the integration of settlers with indigenous people is FEDECAP's stated goal. The Federation represents three substantial farmers' associations near Puyo. FEDECAP does not focus on land rights, which are basic to any indigenous struggle, but rather on alleviation of poverty. Its members are engaged in a constant battle, for example, against the communal land title that was granted to OPIP because they would prefer individual land titles that can be freely bought and sold. In addition, they have fought against bilingual education and in support of oil companies. This is a campesino organization, with economic support from the national campesino organization, FENOC.[20]

Local Government

As in the other provinces, the main government authorities are the mayor, the governor, and the prefect. In Pastaza, the military also plays an important role in governing the region. Political institutions are not very strong, and they tend to be underfinanced, compared with those in the rest of the country. This is a problem for local authorities, as 56 percent of the national budget comes from oil extracted in the Amazon, yet only 4.7 percent goes back to the Amazon region. Roberto de la Torre, Pastaza's prefect, observed, "It does not seem correct that the peoples of the Amazon, surrounded by the most profitable industry in the country, petroleum production, should be surrounded by the most depressing economic misery in the country."[21]

This situation of disproportionate allocation of wealth creates a unique relationship between the provincial and national government. In Bolívar, for example, the local government asks the federal government for economic development assistance and appreciates it in a dependent relationship that could be described as paternalistic. In contrast, the citizens of Pastaza believe that they are giving away their benefits to the rest of the country. In effect, the federal government is taking a great deal of oil income from Pastaza, so it is not surprising that the relationship is often less friendly.

During the early 1990s, the local government of Pastaza appeared sympathetic to the perspective of the indigenous movement. Local officials understood that colonization was destroying traditional indigenous ways of life, the people's interdependence with the environment, and the concept of "territoriality" that the indigenous people were and are still defending. Fausto Espín, governor of Pastaza, said, "It is good that they defend their natural habitat; that is their way of life, and it deserves respect: It is in self-defense that they defend their territory."[22]

At the same time, local governments in the Amazon provinces have a larger objective of developing the region to stimulate the economy. Governor Espín reflected this viewpoint: "I hope that soon some capitalists from other countries will come here to our little province and invest."[23] The aspiration of the current administration in Pastaza is for an oil pipeline to go through the province, which would guarantee a new road and, even more important, jobs.

The Mayor of the canton of Puyo, Patricio López, put in a specific budget request to the central government for development of "marginal" communities because most of his annual budget goes toward maintaining city functions. He has voiced a commitment to respond to the requests of the indigenous communities in the canton. In addition, his office has specific agreements that make physical space available for indigenous organizations. For example, the pan-Amazon indigenous federation, Confederation of Indigenous Nationalities of the Ecuadoran Amazon (CONFENIAE), which has its office in the canton, recently signed a five-year agreement with the city of Puyo to provide an indigenous, traditional medicine pharmacy.

As in the other provinces, development projects in Pastaza are built using volunteer communal work parties (composed of indigenous people) in the rural areas. Mayor López explained, "Without the people's participation, it would be impossible for the government to help them with the scarce resources available to us."[24]

Transportation is one of the most important concerns of the communities. As in all of Ecuador, indigenous people want more effective methods of transporting their products. While Mayor López wanted to respond to their request, he also understood OPIP's concerns:

"The road will be followed by development that will be a step backward for the country because it destroys nature, and it destroys the forest. Beyond that, settlers come and acquire the lands of the Indians, the citizens who have inhabited these lands for hundreds of years."[25]

The indigenous organizations have suggested alternatives to building roads, and the government agreed to sponsor water taxis that would work like buses. Public transportation along the rivers via motor boat (much faster than the canoes at the disposal of most families) should contribute to the resolution of the transportation problem without further destruction of the forest.

Military

The military maintains relations with the communities and their organizations and usually participates in any official dialogue between them and corporate or government representatives. The military engages in active recruitment from indigenous communities in order to create stronger ties and, theoretically, to provide social mobility opportunities for indigenous youth. Some observers, including Governor Espín, see the recruitment of indigenous youth as an ideal way to bring discipline to the communities. Interestingly, indigenous recruitment is also considered a method to prevent "brain drain," as indigenous recruits are more likely to invest their training and income back into their own communities. In addition, the local indigenous communities provide the best soldiers for the Amazon, in contrast to urban youth, who do not adapt well to the environment.

Military recruitment of indigenous people is part of a larger national strategy, the Civic Action Program, aimed at strengthening the national government's relations with the indigenous communities. Started after the 1990 Indigenous Uprising, this program is a nation-building strategy through which indigenous youth are taught to defend and identify with Ecuador, beyond their home communities. A newsletter from the Pastaza Brigade (the Pastaza military base) cites as its number-one goal: "to strengthen the civil-military relations in order to strengthen national unity."[26] Civic action can include development work, ranging from painting a school to building a soccer field, providing rice for an indigenous Congress, and providing medical attention. The plan is also a counter-insurgency effort in which the military does favors for the indigenous organizations and communities while gathering intelligence. "This has allowed us to get closer to the organizations that in the past we couldn't even have had a discussion with," said Colonel de la Rosa of the Pastaza Brigade.[27]

The Civic Action Program is considered "preventive." The actions take place in areas that are sensitive politically and where there could be roots of insurgency (in this case, the indigenous movement). The armed forces of the United States often contribute to the civic actions. "The developed countries no longer need to help us to fight insurrections, but to help prevent them," Colonel de la Rosa explained. "The Ecuadoran Constitution calls on the armed forces not only for defense, but also for the development of the country, in order to secure peace," he added.[28]

Clientelism/Citizenship

The type of clientelism practiced in the Amazon is unique because of local indigenous perceptions of political responsibility and because of the lack of political institutions in the region. In terms of the traditional cultural concepts of power among indigenous people, one of the fundamental responsibilities of a community leader is to guarantee the continual redistribution of wealth in the community. In the Amazon region, outside the large cantons, military troops assigned to civic action duty and missionaries representing various Christian denominations guide development and administer justice, assuming roles that are played by local governments in most other regions of the country.

The primary point of interaction between the indigenous people and the local government is the development of infrastructure. The prefect has established a system in which he works directly with each community, contracting with a local indigenous person(theoretically elected by the community) to manage each project. In this way, the indigenous community becomes the fiscal agent and manager of the project. Understandably, the community manager, who has a contract with the provincial government, is in an enviable position vis-à-vis the community. That individual is likely to go to great lengths to remain in good standing with the provincial government, rather than challenge it, to guarantee the continuity of the contract and the resulting income for the entire indigenous community.

The military maintains a permanent dialogue with OPIP and the other regional organizations, primarily concerning civic action development projects, but it often helps resolve political disputes. By asking for the military's assistance, OPIP leaders claim, they avoid becoming indebted to particular political parties, thus breaking the parties' historic control over indigenous people's access to goods and services. In this way, as in Bolívar, the indigenous organization is taking small but important steps toward citizenship.

LOJA

Background

L oja is unique among the Highlands' provinces. It is located at the southern tip of Ecuador, high in the Andes, in a steep, mountainous region of extreme beauty. In this province, the indigenous people are a minority; but in the cantons of Saraguro and San Lucas, they are the vast majority. The Saraguros are Quichua people. They have few land conflicts, but about half of their population has moved to the neighboring Amazonian province of Zamorra Chinchipe, where, through negotiations with the Shuar Federation, they have occupied land and gained land titles and are engaged in raising cattle and farming. This region was not characterized by feudal farms (haciendas), as was the rest of the Highlands. A few haciendas there continue to be focal points of unresolved land conflicts, but, for the most part, the Saraguros have been self-sufficient. The Saraguros are isolated in three cantons in the north of the province, where they make up a majority of the population (statistical information is not available). Except for interviews with the provincial authorities and some archival research in the capital city of Loja, most of the field research for this study was carried out in the canton of Saraguro.

Provincial Indigenous Organization

The indigenous organizations in Loja were formed in a context of discrimination and political exclusion. The Saraguros maintain a strong, vibrant, independent culture. Compared with the indigenous people in the rest of Ecuador, they remain socially separate, with few marriages outside their nationality despite general economic integration. The Saraguros' perception of the national government is reflected clearly in the report of an annual meeting of their provincial organization: "Instead of suggesting alternatives to improve our living conditions, the government sees the indigenous people as an enemy that must be eliminated."[29] The Saraguros have a high degree of education within their communities due to the presence of an important university nearby in the capital city of Loja.

Saraguros have two organizations in the province: the Inter-provincial Federation of Indigenous Saraguros (Federación Interprovincial de Indígenas Saraguros — FIIS) and the Inter-provincial Coordinator of Indigenous Organizations of Saraguro (Coordinadora Interprovincial de Organizaciones Indígenas Saraguro — CIOIS). The two organizations compete for resources and influence, but in general they share the same ideology. CIOIS is an affiliate of CONAIE, whereas FIIS works more directly with the government. The objectives of the Saraguros' federations were defined as "to strengthen our community organizations as the indigenous people that we are, recognize our own worth, be respected as such, and participate in national civic life."[30]

Most of the leaders of these organizations participated in the adult literacy campaigns sponsored by the Roldós administration and the Catholic University. Bilingual, bicultural education was extremely important in the Saraguro area because most of the adult population had lost the ability to speak their native language. "I remember my grandmother telling me I had to leave Quichua and learn Castilian [Spanish] in order to change the laws," explained an adult literacy campaigner. "Now it appears that there is a new appreciation of our language and our culture among the youth."[31]

The nonindigenous communities in neighboring cantons have asked the Saraguro communities for assistance on a number of occasions. According to local indigenous leaders, mestizos ask for assistance in organizational matters so that they can make the same demands as the indigenous communities on issues such as infrastructure and health care. The only organizational experience the campesinos tend to have is the association of "parents of schoolchildren." Indigenous communities, on the other hand, are demonstrating a model for participation in government decisions by demanding their rights as rural citizens.

The 1990 Indigenous Uprising was highly successful in Loja. As a result, the provincial government and local authorities have started to take indigenous organizations more seriously. According to Manuel Medina of CIOIS, "It was as though the authorities of Loja just realized for the first time that there is an indigenous population in their province, and a well-organized one!"[32]

Local Government

The government authorities in Loja are members of the mestizo urban elite, as in Bolívar. Because the primary interest of this study is indigenous-state relations, most of the research interviews were conducted in the canton of Saraguro, where the majority of the indigenous population reside. Those interviewed included a political chief, a political lieutenant, and a police chief of the canton, all named by the governor. The governor, who officiates from the nearby capital city of Loja, also was interviewed.

The mestizos of Saraguro see the indigenous communities as separatists. Jaime Arias said, "I think the Saraguros are racist toward the whites and mestizos. We are not racist toward them, nor do we see them as below us. They are the ones who close off the circle, who do not want to integrate into the human collective of the province of Loja."[33]

Similarly, the mestizos do not support indigenous demands for indigenous teachers in schools that have a majority indigenous student body, as this would be considered divisive by the authorities. Compared with those of the other two provinces examined in this chapter, the authorities of Saraguro demonstrated little understanding of indigenous ideology and presented an entirely different position — they appeared to be threatened by indigenous demands and resentful of indigenous accusations of racism.

Military

The military presence was noticeably strong in the province of Loja because Loja shares a border with Peru, and Ecuador had a long-standing territorial dispute with that neighboring country. The military is engaged in civic action in the province, as in the rest of the country, with the indigenous communities. The local military commander said, during a ceremony: "The soldier of this brigade has a gun in one hand and a shovel in the other, . . . which means improved development for this province."[34] The political chief of Saraguro asked the national minister of defense to establish a military base in Saraguro for the stated reason of bringing the social benefits of civic action campaigns to her canton. At the time of this writing, a Saraguro base had not been opened.

Clientelism/Citizenship

On the occasion of the 500-year anniversary of the "conquest of the Americas," October 12, 1992, the indigenous communities closed the Pan-American Highway between Saraguro and the provincial capital, Loja, for a week. The paralysis cost the province of Loja upwards of 100 million sucres (at that time, about US$50,000).[35] The mestizo citizens of Saraguro sent a panicked telegram to the governor and the media, claiming that they were running out of basic foods and threatening to take the "necessary measures" to defend themselves. Rather than send in the military, as was done during the 1990 Uprising, the local government sent a delegation, including the governor, the mayor, the health director, and the military commander to negotiate with the indigenous leadership.

Governor Vinicio Suarez responded to every one of the indigenous people's demands, among them: 1) moving a military base out of an indigenous community, 2) replacing government representatives in the cantons, 3) and even writing to the bus cooperative to request the transfer of two drivers accused of racism. In response to the demands that were beyond the governor's authority, he sent letters to the president of the republic.

Despite his attentive response, the governor made clear that closing the road was unacceptable and, in answering a request from the political chief, tried to install a military base in Saraguro "to keep order." At that time, the canton had only four policemen.[36]

The indigenous organizations in Saraguro are identity-based, a factor that is recognized by government officials, and they tend to make demands specific to the needs of the Saraguro people. One local authority stated, "We receive them in the offices, and they ask for the benefits of the modern age, electricity, roads, and such, but they want it for their groups only; they don't think in terms of benefiting the entire canton."[37]

Saraguro has had a few indigenous councilmen, one with the Democratic Left Party (ID) and another with the Ecuadoran Socialist Party (PSE). According to one of those councilmen, as indigenous representatives, they were isolated and powerless. In contrast, an indigenous political lieutenant in one of the cantons was considered very successful and respected.[38] A government representative at that level who is indigenous in an entirely indigenous canton is more qualified to keep the peace, resolve disputes, and interpret the status of social conflicts in order to report accurately to superiors. Most important, community members feel that the representative is *their* authority, rather than that of a "foreign" government.

The indigenous organizations in Saraguro have demanded to have local authorities who will represent their communities, as opposed to the norm, who are local authorities that represent the minister of the national government. By persevering with their demands, the indigenous organizations are provoking changes that serve them as an identity-based collective, which also impact the institutionalized clientelism in the region. An indigenous authority is named not because of a commitment to a political party, nor for having delivered votes for a politician, but on the basis of qualifications — which in this case include an ethnic variable — for keeping the peace. The institutional effect is that such positions now may be filled by persons with qualifications other than the ability to deliver votes.

The possibility always exists that indigenous leaders may trade the votes of their communities to gain government jobs. This exchange can and does happen, although usually for benefits such as buildings, not for political posts to which the indigenous communities have not yet had access.

Using ethnicity as a factor in naming political positions may imply some danger as well. The government authorities of Saraguro will not publicly treat indigenous people in different ways from the other citizens, although there is a context of exclusion, as mentioned. Loja's Governor Suárez, for example, said that treating indigenous people differently would be "fascist," and, accordingly, he had no specific policy or staff for indigenous people. He maintained that he held a strong belief in integration, as did all the local authorities interviewed in that province, and said, "In reality, when the Indian does not integrate into the rest of society, he becomes a weight on that society because he does not produce; he only consumes."[39]

Indigenous communities are not reaching politicians in Loja as they are in Bolívar and Pastaza. Among Loja's authorities, there seems to be little understanding of the indigenous position: No liaisons exist between the government and the communities, and the indigenous organizations have a political perspective that is completely outside the established political system of representation.

CONCLUSION

For democracy to work, citizens must understand that they are citizens, believe that the system is theirs, and see that they will benefit from it if they participate in it. Robert Putnam demonstrates clearly, in his study of the elements of democracy in Italy, that it is not enough to create the institutions of democracy if no active civil society is ready to participate in them.[40] The same universal tenets of democracy can be applied in rural Ecuador. BThis research shows that Ecuador's indigenous population only recently has begun a transformation from "subjects" to "citizens." Roberto de la Torre, a prefect in Pastaza, stated the case clearly:

> The indigenous sector has a profound distrust of the Ecuadoran political leadership, from any party. This is a serious concern because it means that approxi-

mately 40 percent of Ecuadorans do not trust their government, which should be cause for concern for any politician.[41]

This research suggests that contemporary indigenous organizations are impacting the political system not only at the national level but in the countryside as well. In Bolívar and Pastaza, indigenous organizations have had some success in reaching the Hispanic population with their ideology. In those provinces, the local authorities expressed a commitment to the indigenous population, were able to state their concerns, and had hired specific staff to deal with indigenous organizations. The authorities in these two provinces were in a constant dialogue with the indigenous organizations that are important constituents in decisionmaking. In Loja, however, the Saraguro communities had notably less success in breaking through the traditional separation of the two cultures to have their agenda included. They have, however, used their alliance with the national movement to demand changes in local authority structures. Roberto Llerena, prefect of Bolívar, summarized the overall indigenous situation as follows:

> I believe the country of Ecuador is moving forward as a result of the struggle of the indigenous peoples. They have demonstrated that they are a power, they are a force, they are a people who think and have a voice, and they have their aspirations. They are causing changes.[42]

Clearly, material need is an important mobilizing factor, as we have seen in the theoretical debates about social movements, but the ideological context also is necessary for groups to organize as a movement. As the governor of Pastaza in 1993, Fausto Espín of the Liberal Party, said, "What the indigenous do well is organize to defend their rights."

Notes

1. See, for example, the 1990 volume edited by Jonathan Fox, *The Challenge of Rural Democratization: Perspectives from Latin America and the Philippine*s (Portland, Ore.: Frank Cass).

2. Jonathan Fox, 1997, "The Difficult Transition from Clientelism to Citizenship: Lessons from Mexico," in *The New Politics of Inequality in Latin America*, eds. Douglas A. Chalmers, Carlos M. Vilas, Katherine Hite, Scott B. Martin, Kerianne Piester, and Monique Segarra (New York: Oxford University Press), 393.

3. For an economic-based analysis of the indigenous movement, see Luis Fernando Botero, 1992, *Indios, tierra y cultura* (Quito: Abya-Yala); Zamosc 1993; Karovkin 1993; Ibarra 1987; and Silva 1991, among others.

4. Jonathan Fox provides excellent arguments concerning the transformation of rural clientelism to citizenship as an essential factor for democracy in many of his publications. In particular, see Jonathan Fox, 1994, "The Difficult Transition from Clientelism to Citizenship: Lessons from Mexico," *World Politics* 46 (January): 151-184.

5. Jorge Toalombo, 1993, Indigenous Affairs Office of the Prefect, Bolívar, interview by author.

6. This is very gradually changing since the indigenous organization's decision to participate in the electoral process.

7. Jaime Árias, 1993, political intendant, Saraguro, interview by author.

8. These figures, based on the national census of 1990, represent one of the few statistical sources available.

9. Leaders of FECAB (Bolívar Campesino Federation), 1991, interviews by author.

10. Leaders of FECAB, 1991, interviews by author.

11. Examples are Jorge Toalombo and Gonzalo Amagandi.

12. Freddy Espínoza, 1993, mayor of Guaranda, interview by author.

13. Roberto Llerena, 1993, prefect of Bolívar, interview by author.

14. Fox, 1997.

15. Toalombo, 1993, interview by author.

16. International law (such as ILO 169) defines indigenous territory according to "use and occupation."

17. Espín, 1993, interview by author.

18. Villamil, 1993, interview by author.

19. For discussion of the environmental and social impacts of oil extraction in the Ecuadoran Amazon, see Judith Kimmerling, 1991, *Amazon Crude* (New York: Natural Resources Defense Council).

20. Juan Santos, 1993, Campesino Federation of Pastaza, interview by author.

21. Roberto de la Torre, 1993, prefect, Pastaza, interview by author.

22. Espín, 1993, interview by author.

23. Espín, 1993, interview by author.

24. Patricio López, 1993, mayor of Puyo, interview by author.

25. López, 1993, interview by author.

26. Brigada de Selva, 1993, "*Iwia: Informativo de la 17-B.S. Pastaza*" (Newsletter of the Pastaza Brigade), July, Puyo, Ecuador, 9.

27. Colonel de la Rosa 1993, Pastaza Brigade (Pastaza military base), interview by author.

28. Colonel de la Rosa, 1993.

29. CIOIS (Inter-provincial Coordinator of Indigenous Organizations of Saraguro), 1993, "Evaluation of 1992 and Planning of Activities for 1993," report of the CIOIS annual meeting. Discussed with Manuel Medina, 1993, interview by author.

30. Ortega, 1993, interview by author.

31. Ortega, 1993, interview by author.

32. Medina, 1993, interview by author.

33. Árias, 1993, interview by author.

34. *La Crónica*, October 14, 1992, 14.

35. According to the Loja newspaper, *La Crónica*, October 16, 1992, 3.

36. Suárez, 1993, interview by author.

37. Árias, 1993, interview by author.

38. The provincial director of bilingual education, Loja province, 1993, interview by author.

39. Suárez, 1993, interview by author.

40. Robert Putnam, 1993, *Making Democracy Work: Civic Traditions in Modern Italy* (Princeton, N.J.: Princeton University Press).

41. De la Torre, 1993, interview by author.

42. Llerena, 1993, interview by author.

Chapter 7

Conclusions

This book challenges some basic assumptions of current political science literature. Most important, it challenges the supposition that ethnic political mobilization is detrimental to democracy. On the contrary, the indigenous movement is contributing to democratic reforms.

Next, this research challenges the assumption that Latin America is composed of unitary nation-states. Scholars who analyze emerging democracies in Latin America slight the importance of ethnic diversity, and by doing so, they fail to provide insight into the role of ethnicity in Latin American politics. The indigenous movement in Latin America today — from the armed rebellion in Mexico to isolated traditional peoples defending the Amazon rain forests — provides living testimony for the ethnic diversity that survives within each Latin American nation. The political project to construct a world of hegemonic nation-states is no longer adequate.

My analysis of the indigenous movement in Ecuador suggests that ethnic allegiance and national citizenship need not be mutually exclusive. Instead, the assumption should be made that states are pluri-national, and democratic political models should be revised accordingly.

Ethnic mobilization in Ecuador promotes democratic openings. This assertion, based on the research herein, challenges another assumption in political science literature: that ethnic political mobilization is divisive and will lead to violence and undermine state-building initiatives. Ethnic minorities, because they are organizing from the position of a population excluded from decisionmaking, have a basic political demand: *participation*. In promoting political participation for their constituents, ethnic organizations can create openings for the participation of all of civil society. In Ecuador, increased participation was demonstrated at the national level when CONAIE succeeded in gaining access to the government to discuss important issues affecting indigenous peoples, issues such as privatization of the agrarian sector and education policy. This research also revealed increased indigenous participation at the local level, where clientelistic practices have begun to be replaced by representation in decision-making offices.

Why did the indigenous movement experience dramatic success during the period under study? The research for this study suggests the following explanations:

123

1. The nation-building model of development exacerbated the exclusion of indigenous people, creating the context for ethnic mobilization.
2. Democratic reforms created openings for civil society mobilization.
3. The process of bilingual education promoted a new contemporary indigenous ideology around which to unite.
4. Indigenous organizations succeeded in obtaining symbolic and material resources for their communities.

In Ecuador, government policy toward indigenous peoples is marked by the contradictions that evolve from the pursuit of two models. On the one hand, a nation-building model based on cultural integration and modernization still guides government policy. On the other hand, a pluralist model of democracy, one that should promote diversity, has been the stated goal of the government. These two competing paradigms contributed to the conflicts that emerged from the government's policies toward indigenous peoples.

When there is considerable evidence that the state is loyal to more than one ethnic group, it may lead to a stable pluri-national state. In demonstrating its loyalty to all groups through various political actions, not only does a state gain legitimacy, but also the institutional decision-making processes necessary for a stable democratic system may be strengthened. Contrary to arguments in the literature about nation building, and contrary to the literature about Latin American democracy-building processes, ethnic allegiance and national citizenship need not be mutually exclusive.

The indigenous population in Ecuador has been largely excluded from political participation since the Spanish conquest. Despite attempts at mass acculturation, a large percentage of the rural population has maintained a distinct identity. Constitutional reforms for the first time brought suffrage to indigenous citizens, but they already had established a separate identity within the Ecuadoran nation. Populist governments responded to cultural demands, such as bilingual education, while remaining less responsive to economic demands such as land rights. Now, I suggest, cultural demands have created the most important social movement in Ecuador. Cultural gains provided the resources for the indigenous movement to build a contemporary indigenous identity around which to mobilize.

The bilingual literacy campaigns and, later, the bilingual education process created a new ideology among indigenous people. This ideology is the basis of what can be understood as a counter-hegemonic ethnic movement. Through its demands at the provincial level, the indigenous movement challenges the system of political clientelism that dominates in the countryside, opening the way for citizenship. Through bilingual education and the identity-based tactics of CONAIE, the indigenous movement has reinvented what it means to be "Indian." Beyond the development of an ideology, the indigenous movement has brought about concrete changes in the political system, as exemplified in at least two cases described in Chapter 4, bilingual education and agrarian reform.

The indigenous movement in Ecuador is both a "new social movement" based on identity and a form of collective action based on resource mobilization. Ethnicity is both an ideology in terms of collective identity and a resource used for mobilization of a group in civil society. Considering their exclusion, as indigenous people, from national politics, identity is probably the indigenous population's most important resource. The interplay between ethnicity as an ideology and ethnicity as a resource defines the political sphere.

Changes in the political system that were inspired by the indigenous movement can be observed not only at the national level, but also at the local level. For democracy to work, citizens must understand that they are citizens, believe that the system is theirs, and see that they will benefit from it if they participate in it. It is not enough to create the institutions of democracy if there is no active civil society to participate in it. Based on this research, it is evident that in rural Ecuador the indigenous population is beginning a transformation from "subject" to "citizen."[1]

To present a uniformly positive picture of the indigenous movement in Ecuador would be unrealistic. The movement is wracked by internal strife

*Nina Pacari, an attorney and CONAIE leader,
is now a representative in Ecuador's Congress.*

and by conflicts between "traditional" and "modern" practices, which restrain its development. Differences between the Highlands' and the Amazon's indigenous groups constantly cause strain within the movement. Strategically, because the CONAIE leadership is focused on gaining political space, it does not always prioritize the needs of the local indigenous communities, leaving CONAIE open to criticism. Concurrently, while Ecuador is peaceful compared with its neighbors, it should not be considered a stable democracy, according to most analysts.[2] The current intervention of indigenous communities in national politics is a radical break with their not too distant past behavior as "submissive Indians." That radical break can be understood in terms of the development of a contemporary indigenous movement challenging exclusion from political society.

This research on contemporary indigenous politics in Ecuador leads to further questions that need investigation. More detailed observation of the changing patron-client relationships in rural Ecuador could be a key for understanding the move toward citizenship. The move into electoral politics represents another new phase of the indigenous movement in Ecuador that is ripe for study. Important information can be analyzed regarding the increasing international influence on the movement, including international development assistance and support from the human rights and environmentalist communities.[3] Questions remain as to what is unique about the indigenous movement in relation to other identity-based movements. Are its lessons applicable to other groups? Can other identity-based movements discover a unifying ideology around which to mobilize? Why, for example, has the women's movement in Ecuador had limited success compared with the indigenous movement? Future discussion of political change in Latin America should consider the political significance of identity-based political movements and the political, social, and economic factors that benefit or constrain them. On the broader issues of democratization and national unity, it will be interesting to observe the role of ethnonationalist movements in democratizing countries, particularly concerning questions of citizenship. Finally, research is needed to compare pluri-national models now functioning with indigenous people in Latin America, in order to move toward definition of the variables that describe multi-ethic political systems.

The contemporary indigenous movement in Latin America is capitalizing on political exclusion to strengthen the unity of indigenous peoples. Having developed a contemporary indigenous identity, indigenous leaders built a political movement by demanding rights that constitute demands for citizenship. Through their relatively new organizations, indigenous communities demand inclusion — participation as citizens — with respect for their specific needs as indigenous people. Ecuadoran indigenous organizations are forging a participatory political model that may lead to democratic institutions becoming responsive to the multiethnic nature of their country.

The pluri-national model is relevant to the governments of all ethnically diverse societies. Political science debates about Latin America have largely ignored the issue of ethnic diversity. My contention is that ethnic political movements may contribute to the development of the participatory citizenship that is essential to democracy, as demonstrated by the indigenous organizations in Ecuador.

Quichua students can now study in their own language.

Notes

1. I borrow this phrase from Jorge León. See León 1994.

2. See, for example, Osvaldo Hurtado, 1985, *Political Power in Ecuador* (Boulder, Colo.: Westview Press); and Corkill and Cubitt 1988.

3. Some of this information is available. See, for example, Brysk 2000; and Margaret Keck and Kathryn Sikkink, 1998, *Activists Beyond Borders: Transnational Advocacy Networks in International Politics* (Ithaca, N.Y.: Cornell University Press).

Appendix 1

List of Acronyms

CFP Concentration of Popular Forces (Concentración de Fuerzas Populares)

CIEI Center for the Investigation of Indigenous Education (Centro de Investigaciones para la Educación Indígena)

CIOIS Inter-provincial Coordinator of Indigenous Organizations of Saraguro (Coordinadora Interprovincial de Organizaciones Indígenas de Saraguro)

CODENPE Development Council of Nationalities and Peoples of Ecuador (Consejo de Desarrollo de las Nacionalidades y Pueblos del Ecuador)

CONAIE Confederation of Indigenous Nationalities of Ecuador (Confederación de las Nacionalidades Indígenas del Ecuador)

CONFENIAE Confederation of Indigenous Nationalities of the Ecuadoran Amazon (Confederación de Nacionalidades Indígenas de la Amazonia Ecuatoriana)

CRIC Regional Indigenous Council of Cauca (Consejo Regional Indígena del Cauca)

DINASI National Directorate of Indigenous Health (Dirección Nacional de Salud Indígena)

DINEIB National Directorate of Bilingual Intercultural Education (Dirección Nacional de Educación Intercultural Bilingüe)

DP Popular Democracy Party (Democracia Popular)

ECUARUNARI "Ecuador Runacunapac Riccharimui" (Ecuador Indians Awaken — the Highlands Indigenous Federation)

FADI Broad Front of the Democratic Left (Frente Amplio de Izquierda)

FECAB Bolívar Campesino Federation (Federación Campesina de Bolívar)

FEDECAP Colonist Federation of Pastaza (Federación de Colonos de Pastaza)

FEI Indigenous Federation of Ecuador (Federación Indígena del Ecuador)

Acronyms —continued

FENOC   National Federation of Campesino Organizations (Federación Nacional de Organizaciones Campesinas)

FENOC-I   National Federation of Campesino and Indigenous Organizations (Federación Nacional de Organizaciones Campesinas e Indígenas)

FENOCIN   National Federation of Campesinos, Indigenous, and Negro Organizations (Federación Nacional de Organizaciones Campesinas, Indígenas, y Negras)

FICI   Indigenous Federation of Imbabura (Federación Indígena de Imbabura)

FIIS   Inter-provincial Federation of Indigenous Saraguros (Federación Interprovincial de los Indígenas Saraguros)

FOIN   Federation of Indigenous Organizations of Napo (Federación de Organizaciones Indígenas del Napo)

FRN   National Reconstruction Front Party (Frente Nacional de Reconstrucción)

FUT   United Workers Front (Frente Unitario de Trabajadores)

ID   Democratic Left (Izquierda Democrática)

IERAC   Ecuadoran Institute for Agrarian Reform and Colonization (Instituto Ecuatoriano de Reforma Agraria y Colonización)

INDA   National Agrarian Development Institute (Instituto Nacional de Desarrollo Agropecuario)

MICH   Indigenous Movement of Chimborazo (Movimiento Indígena de Chimborazo)

MPD   Popular Democratic Movement Party (Movimiento Popular Democrático)

ONIC   National Indigenous Organization of Colombia (Organización Nacional Indígena de Colombia)

OPIP   Organization of Indigenous Peoples of Pastaza (Organización de Pueblos Indígenas de Pastaza)

Proyecto EBI   Indigenous Movement of Chimborazo, Bilingual Intercultural Education Project (Proyecto de Educación Bilingüe Intercultural)

PSC   Social Christian Party (Partido Social Cristiano)

PSE   Ecuadoran Socialist Party (Partido Socialista Ecuatoriano)

Appendix 2

Chronology

Date	Event	Comments
1979-1981	Jaime Roldós administration (DP)	End of military rule; Roldós dies in accident; adult literacy programs
1981-1984	Osvaldo Hurtado administration (MPD)	Roldós's vice president; economic austerity
1984-1988	León Febres Cordero administration (FRN)	"Strongman"
1988-1992	Rodrigo Borja administration (ID)	CONAIE obtains legal status; bilingual education system
June 1990	Indigenous Uprising	Indigenous movement to forefront
1992-1996	Sixto Durán administration (PSC)	Administers privatization policies
1994	Agrarian reform protests	Challenge to privatization policies
1997	President Abdala Bucarám ousted	CONAIE leads civil society protests
January 2000	President Jamil Mahuad ousted	Indigenous/military coup

Appendix 3

List of Formal Interviews

Note: Some names are withheld by request.

INTERVIEWS IN 1991

National Indigenous Leaders:
Alberto Andrango, FENOC-I
Miguel Ángel Carlosamán, FICI
Indigenous Federation of Saraguro
Ampam Karakras (Shuar), director of finances, CONAIE
Miguel Lluco (Chimborazo), ECUARUNARI
Luis Macas (Quichua), president, CONAIE
Fabián Muenala, CONAIE
Humberto Muenala (Otavalo), Proyecto EBI
María Paca (Quichua), MICH, Proyecto EBI
Melecio Santos, CONAIE
Leonardo Viteri (Quichua/Amazon), CONAIE

Scholars:
Iliana Almeida, anthropologist
Alicia Ibarra, sociologist

Government:
Alfonso Calderón, architect, Borja administration
Leonardo Calderón, Borja administration
Luis Luna Gaybor, IERAC
Gonzalo Ortiz, minister of government, Borja administration

Indigenous Communities:
Cabildos of two communities in Guamote, Chimborazo
Federation of Cabildos of Cacha (Federación de Cabildos de Cacha)
Bolívar Campesino Federation (Federación Campesina de Bolívar — FECAB)
Indigenous Movement of Chimborazo (MICH)

INTERVIEWS IN 1993

Government:
Osvaldo Hurtado, former president of Ecuador
José Quimbo, Indigenous Affairs Office of President Sixto Durán Ballén

National Indigenous Leaders:
Luis Macas, president, CONAIE
Nina Pacari, CONAIE
Rafael Pandam, CONAIE
Carmen Porrate, CONAIE

Bilingual Education:
Tránsito Chela, Directorate of Bilingual Intercutural Education
Juan Jigalo, secretary of health, CONAIE
Luis Monteluisa, director, Directorate of EBI
Humberto Muenala, EBI
Luis de la Torre, EBI

Loja Province:
Tayta Alvino Macas, community elder, el Gañil
Jaime Árias, political intendant, Saraguro
Enrique Luzuriaga, police chief, Saraguro
Manuel Medina, CIOIS
Elías Narricella, community leader, Chacaputo
Samuel Ortega, FIIS
Political chief, Saraguro
Fernando Sarango, provincial director of bilingual education
Vinicio Suárez, governor

Bolívar Province:
Gonzalo Amagandi, Campesino Federation of Pastaza
Juan Arévalo, FECAB
Silvana Jaramillo, governor
Community, Bramadero
Community, El Inca

FECAB leadership

Freddy Espinoza, mayor of Guaranda

Roberto Llerena, prefect

María Paca, EBI, CONAIE

Jorge Toalombo, Indigenous Affairs Office of the Prefect, Bolívar

Pastaza Province:

Fausto Espín, governor

Camilo Huatatoca, community of Santa Clara

Patricio López, mayor of Puyo

Colonel de la Rosa, Pastaza military base

Juan Santos, Campesino Federation of Pastaza

Roberto de la Torre, prefect

Antonio Vargas, OPIP, provincial director of bilingual education

Luis Vargas, ex-president of CONFENIAE, president of Achuar Association

Hector Villamil, president, OPIP

Lukas Yasacamán, community of San Lucas

Appendix 4

CONAIE Demands to the Government, 1990 Uprising: The Pluri-National Mandate

1. Declaration of Ecuador as a pluri-national state.

2. The return of lands and the legalization of territories for the indigenous peoples, without costly legal fees.

3. Sufficient water for both human consumption and irrigation in the indigenous communities and an environmental plan to prevent the contamination of water supplies.

4. Debt pardon for all debts indigenous communities have incurred with government ministries and banks.

5. A minimum two-year price freeze on all raw materials and manufactured goods used by the communities in agricultural production and a reasonable price increase for all agricultural products sold by the communities.

6. No payment of the municipal taxes levied on the small properties owned by indigenous farmers.

7. Creation of long-term financing for bilingual education programs in the communities.

8. Creation of provincial and regional credit agencies under the control of CONAIE.

9. Immediate delivery of funds and credits currently assigned to the indigenous nationalities.

10. Initiation and termination of all necessary and priority construction of basic infrastructure in the indigenous communities.

11. Unrestricted import and export privileges for indigenous artisans and merchants of artisan crafts.

12. National legislation and enforcement of strict protection and controlled exploration of archeological sites under supervision of CONAIE.

13. Expulsion of Summer Institute of Linguistics from the Amazon in accordance with Executive Decree 1159 of 1981.

14. Respect for the rights of children and the raising of consciousness in the government regarding the actual state of affairs among children.

15. National support for the practice of indigenous medicine.

16. Immediate dismantling of organizations created by political parties that parallel governmental institutions at the provincial and municipal levels and that manipulate political consciousness and elections in indigenous communities.

References

Almeida, José. 1993. "El levantamiento indígena como momento constitutivo nacional." In *Sismo étnico en el Ecuador: Varias perspectivas*, ed. CEDIME (Centro de Investigaciones de los Movimientos Sociales del Ecuador). Quito: Abya-Yala.

Álvarez, Sonia E., Evelina Dagnino, and Arturo Escobar. 1998. *Cultures of Politics, Politics of Cultures: Revisioning Latin America's Social Movements*. Boulder, Colo.: Westview Press.

Andean Commission of Jurists. 1990. "Demandas Indígenas." *Informativo Andino* 44 (July 16).

Anderson, Benedict. 1983. *Imagined Communities: Reflections on the Origins and Spread of Nationalism*. London: Verso.

Anderson, Lisa. 1987. "The State in the Middle East and North Africa." *Comparative Politics* 20 (1): 1-18.

Andolina, Robert. 1998. "CONAIE (and Others) in the Ambiguous Spaces of Democracy: Positioning for the 1997-1998 Asemblea Nacional Constituyente in Ecuador." Paper for the Latin American Studies Association (LASA).

Andrango, Alberto. 1991. FENOC-I. Interview by author.

Arévalo, Juan. 1993. Bolívar Campesino Federation (Federación Campesina de Bolívar — FECAB). Interview by author.

Árias, Jaime. 1993. Political intendent, Saraguro. Interview by author.

Ayala Mora, Enrique. 1989. *Los partidos políticos en el Ecuador*. Quito: Ediciones la Tierra.

Barsky, Osvaldo. 1988. *La Reforma Agraria Ecuatoriana*. Quito: Corporación Editora Nacional.

Bebbington, Anthony, Galo Ramón, Hernán Carrasco, Víctor Hugo Torres, Lourdes Peralvo, and Jorge Trujillo. 1992. *Actores de una década ganada: Tribus, comunidades, y campesinos en la modernidad*. Quito: Communidec.

Bebbington, Anthony, Galo Ramón, Hernán Carrasco, Víctor Hugo Torres, Lourdes Peralvo, and Jorge Trujillo. 1992. "De la protesta a la productividad: Evolución de las federaciones indígenas del Ecuador." *Desarrollo de Base* 16 (2): 11-21.

Belote, Linda, and Jim Belote. 1984. "Drain from the Bottom: Individual Ethnic Identity Change in Southern Ecuador." *Social Forces* 63 (1).

Bloom, William. 1990. *Personal Identity, National Identity, and International Relations*. New York: Cambridge University Press.

Bonilla, Adrián. 1993. "Internal Security and Society: Are We in Danger?" *Hoy* April 25.

Botasso, Juan, ed. 1986. *Del indigenismo a las organizaciones indígenas*. Quito: Abya-Yala.

Botero, Luis Fernando. 1992. *Indios, tierra y cultura*. Quito: Abya-Yala.

Bourdieu, Pierre. 1989. "What Makes a Social Class? On the Theoretical and Practical Existence of Groups." *Berkeley Journal of Sociology* 32: 1-18.

Breuilly, John. 1985. *Nationalism and the State*. Manchester, U.K.: Manchester University Press.

Brigada de Selva. 1993. *"Iwia: Informativo de la 17-B.S. Pastaza"* (Newsletter of the Pastaza Brigade). July. Puyo, Ecuador.

Bright, Charles, and Susan Harding. 1984. *State-making and Social Movements.* Ann Arbor, Mich.: University of Michigan Press.

Brysk, Alison. 1994. "Acting Globally: Indian Rights and International Politics in Latin America." In *Indigenous Peoples and Democracy in Latin America*, ed. Donna Van Cott. New York: St. Martin's Press.

Brysk, Alison. 2000. *From Tribal Village to Global Village: Indian Rights and International Relations in Latin America.* Stanford, Calif.: Stanford University Press.

Carlosamán, Miguel Ángel. 1991. Indigenous Federation of Imbabura (Federción Indígena y Campesina de Imbabura — FICI). Interview by author.

CEDIME (Centro de Documentación y Información de Movimientos Ecuatorianos). 1993. *Sismo étnico en el Ecuador: Varias perspectivas.* Quito: Abya-Yala.

CEPLAES (Centro de Planificación y Estudios Sociales). 1996. *Proyecto de Investigación Pueblos Indígenas y Participación Electoral: Informe Final.* Quito.

CIDCA (Centro de Información y Documentación de la Costa Atlántica). 1987. *Ethnic Groups and the Nation-State: The Case of the Atlantic Coast in Nicaragua.* Stockholm: University of Stockholm.

CIOIS (Inter-provincial Coordinator of Indigenous Organizations of Saraguro—Coordinadora Interprovincial de Organizaciones Indígenas Saraguro). 1993. *Evaluation of 1992 and Planning of Activities for 1993.* Report of the CIOIS annual meeting.

Chela, Tránsito. 1993. Directorate of Bilingual Education. Interview by author.

Chiriboga, Manuel. 1986. "Crisis económica y movimiento campesino e indígena." In *Movimientos sociales en el Ecuador*, eds. Centro Andino de Acción Popular. Quito: CAAP.

Churchill, Ward, ed. 1983. *Marxism and Native Americans.* Boston: South End Press.

Cohen, Jean. 1985. "Strategy or Identity." *Social Research* 52:4 (Winter).

CONAIE (Conferación de las Nacionalidades Indígenas del Ecuador). 1989. *Las nacionalidades indígenas en el Ecuador: Nuestro proceso organizativo.* Quito: Abya-Yala.

CONAIE. 1994. *El Estado Plurinacional.* Quito: Impreso CONAIE.

CONAIE Bulletin. 1993. March 9.

Connor, Walker. 1972. "Nation-building or Nation-destroying?" *World Politics* 24 (3): 319-355.

Connor, Walker. 1984. "Eco- or Ethno-nationalism." *Ethnic and Racial Studies* 7 (3): 342-359.

Connor, Walker. 1987. "Ethnonationalism." In *Understanding Political Development: An Analytic Study*, eds. Myron Weiner and Samuel P. Huntington. Boston: Little, Brown.

Congressional Research Service. 1991. *Latin America's Indigenous Peoples and Considerations for U.S. Assistance.* #91-663 F.

Corkill, David, and David Cubitt. 1988. *Ecuador: Fragile Democracy.* London: Latin America Bureau (Research and Action).

Cornejo Menacho, Diego. 1991. *INDIOS: Una reflexión sobre el Levantamiento Indígena de 1990.* Quito: Logos.

Cornejo Menacho, Diego. 1993. *Los indios y el Estado-País: Pluriculturalidad y multietnicidad en el Ecuador: Contribuciones al debate.* Quito: Abya-Yala.

Corporación de Estudios y Publicaciones. Updated in 1993. *Leyes Reforma Agraria; Colonización de la Región Amazónica; Tierras Baldías y Colonización; y Reglamentos.* Quito.

Corporación Editora Nacional, ed. 1992. *Pueblos Indios, Estado y Derecho.* Quito: Abya-Yala.

Crain, Mary. 1990. "The Social Construction of National Identity in Highland Ecuador." *Anthropological Quarterly* 63 (1): 43-59.

de la Torre, Roberto. 1993. Prefect of Pastaza. Interview by author.

Deutsch, Karl. 1962. *Nationalism and Social Communication.* Cambridge, Mass.: MIT Press.

Díaz-Polanco, Héctor. 1987. "*Neoindigenismo* and the Ethnic Question in Central America." *Latin American Perspectives* 14 (1).

Eagleton, Terry. 1991. *Ideology: An Introduction.* New York: Verso Books.

Eckstein, Susan, ed. 1989. *Power and Popular Protest.* Berkeley, Calif.: University of California Press.

ECUARUNARI (Ecuador Runacunapac Riccharimui), ed. 1989. *Nuestra voz, Nuestra cultura: Taller Andino de Intercambio de Experiencias en Educación y Comunicación de Organizaciones Campesino-Indígenas.* Quito: ECUARUNARI.

Ehrenreich, Jeffrey. 1985. *Political Anthropology of Ecuador: Perspectives from Indigenous Cultures.* Albany, N.Y.: State University of New York at Albany.

El Universo. 1991. March 4.

Enloe, Cynthia. 1981. "The Growth of the State and Ethnic Mobilization." *Ethnic and Racial Studies* 4 (2): 123-136.

Escobar, Arturo, and Sonia Álvarez, eds. 1992. *The Making of Social Movements in Latin America.* Boulder, Colo.: Westview Press.

Espín, Fausto. 1993. Governor of Pastaza province. Interview by author.

Espinoza, Freddy. 1993. Mayor of Guaranda. Interview by author.

Federación de Cabildos de Cacha (Cacha Federation of Town Halls). 1991. Interview by author.

Foucault, Michel. 1980. *Power and Knowledge.* New York: Pantheon Books.

Fox, Jonathan. 1990. *The Challenge of Rural Democratization: Perspectives from Latin America and the Philippines.* Portland, Ore.: Frank Cass.

Fox, Jonathan. 1994a. Latin America's Emerging Local Politics." *Journal of Democracy* 5 (2): 105-16.

Fox, Jonathan. 1994b. "The Difficult Transition from Clientelism to Citizenship: Lessons from Mexico." *World Politics* 46 (January): 151-184.

Fox, Jonathan. 1996. "How Does Civil Society Thicken? The Political Construction of Social Capital in Rural Mexico." *World Development* 24 (6): 1089-1103.

Fox, Jonathan. 1997. "The Difficult Transition from Clientelism to Citizenship: Lessons from Mexico. In *The New Politics of Inequality in Latin America*, eds. Douglas A. Chalmers, Carlos M. Vilas, Katherine Hite, Scott B. Martin, Kerianne Piester, and Monique Segarra. New York: Oxford University Press.

Frank, Erwin, Nina Patiño, and Marta Rodríguez. 1992 . *Los políticos y los indígenas.* Quito: Abya-Yala/ILDIS (Instituto Latinoamericano de Investigaciones Sociales).

Geertz, Clifford. 1973. *The Interpretation of Cultures.* New York: Basic Books.

Gellner, Ernest. 1983. *Nations and Nationalism.* Ithaca, N.Y.: Cornell University Press.

Geuss, Raymond. 1981. *The Idea of Critical Theory: Habermas and the Frankfurt School.* New York: Cambridge University Press.

Glazer, Nathan, and Daniel Moynihan. 1975. *Ethnicity: Theory and Experience.* Cambridge, Mass.: Harvard University Press.

Gramsci, Antonio. 1971. *Selections from the Prison Notebooks of Antonio Gramsci.* New York: International.

Grijalva, Agustín. 1994. *Datos Básicos de la Realidad Nacional.* Quito: Corporación Editora Nacional.

Guerrero, Andrés. 1993. "La desintegración de la administración étnica en el Ecuador." In *Sismo étnico en el Ecuador: Varias perspectivas,* ed. CEDIME (Centro de Investigaciones de los Movimientos Sociales del Ecuador). Quito: Abya-Yala.

Gurr, Ted R. 1969. *Why Men Rebel.* Princeton, N.J.: Princeton University Press.

Hale, Charles. 1987. "Inter-Ethnic Relations and Class Structure in Nicaragua's Atlantic Coast." In *Ethnic Groups and the Nation-State: The Case of the Atlantic Coast in Nicaragua,* by The Center for Investigation and Documentation of the Atlantic Coast (Centro de Información y Documentación de la Costa Atlántica — CIDA). Stockholm: University of Stockholm.

Hale, Charles. 1994. *Resistance and Contradiction: Miskitu Indians and the Nicaraguan State, 1894-1987.* Stanford, Calif.: Stanford University Press.

Harvey, Neil. 1999. *The Chiapas Rebellion: The Struggle for Land and Democracy.* Durham, N.C.: Duke University Press.

Hendricks, Janet. 1991. "Symbolic Counterhegemony Among the Ecuadoran Shuar." In *Nation-States and Indians in Latin America,* eds. Greg Urban and Steven Scherzer. Austin, Texas: University of Texas Press.

Hobsbawm, E. J. 1990. *Nations and Nationalism since 1780: Programme, myth, reality.* New York: Cambridge University Press.

Horowitz, Donald. 1985. *Ethnic Groups in Conflict.* Berkeley, Calif.: University of California Press.

Hoy. 1993. June 24.

Hurtado, Osvaldo. 1985. *Political Power in Ecuador.* Boulder, Colo.: Westview Press.

Hurtado, Osvaldo. 1993. *Gobernabilidad y reforma constitutional.* Quito: Corporación Editora Nacional.

Ibarra, Alicia. 1991. Sociologist working in the office of President Jaime Roldós. Interview by the author.

Ibarra, Alicia, ed. 1987. *Los indígenas y el Estado en el Ecuador.* Quito: Abya-Yala.

Jelin, Elizabeth, ed. 1990. *Women and Social Change in Latin America.* London: United Nations Research Institute and Zed Books.

Karakras, Ampam. 1991. Shua, director of finances for CONAIE.

Karl, Terry. 1987. "Petroleum and Political Pacts: The Transition to Democracy in Venezuela." In *Transitions from Authoritarian Rule: Latin America,* eds. Guillermo O'Donnell, Philippe C. Schmitter, and Laurence Whitehead. Baltimore: The Johns Hopkins University Press.

Karovkin, Tanya. 1993. *Indians, Peasants, and the State: The Growth of a Community Movement in the Ecuadoran Andes.* Occasional Paper No. 3. Ontario: York University, CERLAC (Center for Research on Latin America and the Caribbean).

Katznelson, Ira. 1972. "Comparative Studies of Race and Ethnicity." *Comparative Politics* (October): 135-154.

Keck, Margaret, and Kathryn Sikkink. 1998. *Activists Beyond Borders: Transnational Advocacy Networks in International Politics*. Ithaca, N.Y.: Cornell University Press.

Kellas, James. 1991. *The Politics of Nationalism and Ethnicity*. New York: St. Martin's Press.

Kimmerling, Judith. 1991. *Amazon Crude* (New York: Natural Resources Defense Council).

Kotkin, Joel. 1992. *Tribes*. New York: Random House.

Laclau, Ernesto, and Chantal Mouffe. 1985. *Hegemony and Socialist Strategy: Towards a Radical Democratic Politics*. London: Verso.

La Crónica. 1992. October 14.

La Crónica. 1992. October 16.

León, Jorge. 1990. "Levantamiento indígena, levantamiento campesino: Actores, propuestas, contexto, perspectivas." Unpublished text of paper given on July 5 at FLACSO (Facultad Latino Americana de Ciencias Sociales).

León, Jorge. 1994. *De campesinos a ciudadanos diferentes*. Quito: CEDIME (Centro de Investigaciones de los Movimientos Sociales del Ecuador).

Lijphart, Arend. 1977. *Democracy in Plural Societies*. New Haven, Conn.: Yale University Press.

Lind, Amy C. 1995. "Gender Development and Women's Political Practices in Ecuador." Ph.D. diss., Cornell University, New York.

Llerena, Roberto. 1993. Prefect, Bolívar. Interview by author.

Lluco, Miguel. 1991. ECUARUNARI leader for Chimborazo. Interview by author.

Luna Gaybor, Luis. 1991. Director of IERAC (Instituto Ecuatoriano de Reforma Agraria y Colonización). Interview by author.

Macas, Luis. 1991. "El levantamiento indígena visto por sus protagonistas." In *INDIOS: Una reflexión sobre el Levantamiento Indígena de 1990*, ed. Diego Cornejo Menacho. Quito: Logos.

Macas, Luis. 1993. Interview by author.

MacNamara, Robert. 1995. *In Retrospect*. New York: Random House.

Maldonado, Luis. 1992. "El movimiento indígena y la propuesta multinacional." In *Pueblos Indio, Estado y Derecho*, ed. Corporación Editora Nacional (Quito: Abya-Yala), 151-163.

Maldonado, Luis. 1993. "Indígenas y Elecciones 1992." In *Sismo étnico en el Ecuador: Varias perspectivas*, ed. CEDIME (Centro de Investigaciones de los Movimientos Sociales del Ecuador). Quito: Abya-Yala, 305-326.

Mallon, Florencia E. 1992. "Indian Communities, Political Cultures, and the State in Latin America, 1780-1990." *Journal of Latin American Studies* 24 (Quincentenary Supplement 1992).

Mariategui, José Carlos. 1925. "El rostro y el alma del Tahuantinsuyo." *Mundial* 6 (274).

Medina, Manuel. 1993. CIOIS (Coordinadora Interprovincial de Organizaciones Indígenas de Saraguro). Interview by author.

Melluci, Alberto. 1984. "An End to Social Movements?" *Social Science Information* 23 (4/5): 819-835.

Moncagatta, Juan Pablo. 1993. Op-ed article. *Hoy*, June 2.

Monteluisa, Luis. 1993. Director, Directorate of Bilingual Intercultural Education. Interview by author.

Moore, Barrington, Jr. 1966. *Social Origins of Dictatorship and Democracy*. Boston: Beacon Press.

Moreno Yánez, Segundo, and José Figueroa. 1992. *El Levantamiento Indígena del Inti-Raymi*. Quito: Abya-Yala.

Motyl, Alexander. 1990. *Sovietology, Rationality, Nationality*. New York: Columbia University Press.

Motyl, Alexander. 1992. "The Modernity of Nationalism." *Journal of International Affairs* 45 (2): 307-323.

Moynihan, Daniel P. 1993. *Pandemonium: Ethnicity and International Politics*. New York: Oxford University Press.

Muenala, Fabián. 1991. Indigenous intellectual at CONAIE. Interview by author.

Muenala, Humberto. 1993. Bilingual Intercultural Education Project. Interview by author.

Munck, Gerardo. 1991. "Social Movements and Democracy in Latin America: Theoretical Debates and Comparative Perspectives." Paper for the April Latin American Studies Association (LASA) conference.

Nash, June. 1989. "Cultural Resistance and Class Consciousness in Bolivian Tin-Mining Communities." In *Power and Popular Protest,* ed. Susan Eckstein. Berkeley, Calif.: University of California Press.

Newman, Saul. 1991. "Does Modernization Breed Ethnic Political Conflict?" *World Politics* 43 (3): 451-478.

Nieto, Santiago. 1993. "El problema indígena." In *Los indios y el Estado-País*, ed. Diego Cornejo Menacho. Quito: Abya-Yala.

O'Donnell, Guillermo, Philippe C. Schmitter, and Laurence Whitehead, eds. 1987a. *Transitions from Authoritarian Rule: Latin America*. Baltimore: The Johns Hopkins University Press.

O'Donnell, Guillermo, Philippe C. Schmitter, and Laurence Whitehead, eds. 1987b. *Transitions from Authoritarian Rule: Comparative Perspectives*. Baltimore: The Johns Hopkins University Press.

Olson, Mancur, Jr. 1965. *The Logic of Collective Action*. Cambridge, Mass.: Harvard University Press.

Omni, Michael, and Howard Winant. 1986. *Racial Formation in the United States*. New York: Routledge & Kegan Paul, Inc.

Ortiz, Roxanne Dunbar. 1984. *Indians of the Americas: Human Rights and Self-Determination*. London: Zed Press.

Ortiz Crespo, Gonzalo. 1991. "El problema indígena y el gobierno." In *INDIOS: Una reflexión sobre el Levantamiento Indígena de 1990*, ed. Diego Cornejo Menacho. Quito: Logos.

Ortiz Crespo, Gonzalo. 1991. Minister of Government. Interview by author.

Paca, María. 1993. Bilingual Education Project, CONAIE. Interview by author.

Paige, Jeffrey. 1975. *Agrarian Revolution*. New York: Free Press.

Popkin, Samuel. 1979. *The Rational Peasant*. Berkeley, Calif.: University of California Press.

Przeworski, Adam. 1988. "Some Problems in the Study of the Transition to Democracy." In *Transitions from Authoritarian Rule: Comparative Perspectives*, eds. Guillermo O'Donnell, Philippe C. Schmitter, and Laurence Whitehead. Baltimore: The Johns Hopkins University Press.

Putnam, Robert. 1993. *Making Democracy Work: Civic Traditions in Modern Italy.* Princeton, N.J.: Princeton University Press.

Quimbo, José. 1993. Indigenous Affairs Office of President Sixto Durán Ballén, interview by author.

Rothschild, Joseph. 1981. *Ethnopolitics.* New York: Columbia University Press.

Rothschild, Joseph. 1990. *East Central Europe between the Two World Wars.* Seattle: University of Washington Press.

Rustow, Dankwart. 1970. "Transitions to Democracy." *Comparative Politics* (April): 337-363.

Salomon, Frank. 1982. "The Andean Contrast." *Journal of International Affairs* 36 (1).

Sánchez Parga, José. 1990. *Etnia, poder y diferencia.* Quito: Abya-Yala.

Sánchez Parga, José. 1993. *Transformaciones culturales y educación indígena.* Quito: CAAP (Centro Andino de Acción Popular).

Santana, Roberto. 1995. *Ciudadanos en la etnicidad: Los indios en la política o la política de los indios.* Quito: Abya-Yala.

Santos, Melecio. 1991. Vice-president of CONAIE. Interview by author.

Scott, James C. 1976. *The Moral Economy of the Peasant.* New Haven, Conn.: Yale University Press.

Scott, James C. 1977. "Hegemony and the Peasantry." *Politics and Society* 7 (3): 267-296.

Scott, James C. 1985. *Weapons of the Weak.* New Haven, Conn.: Yale University Press.

Selverston, Melina. 1993. "The 1990 Indigenous Uprising in Ecuador: Politicized Ethnicity as Social Movement." Papers on Latin America #32. Institute of Latin American and Iberian Studies, Columbia University.

Selverston, Melina. 1995. "The Politics of Culture: Indigenous Peoples and the State in Ecuador." In *Indigenous Peoples and Democracy in Latin America,* ed. Donna Van Cott. New York: St. Martin's Press.

Selverston, Melina. 1997a. "The Politics of Identity Reconstruction: Indians and Democracy in Ecuador." In *The New Politics of Inequality in Latin America: Rethinking Participation and Representation,* eds. Douglas A. Chalmers, Carlos M. Vilas, Katherine Hite, Scott B. Martin, Kerianne Piester, and Monique Segarra. New York: Oxford University Press.

Selverston-Scher, Melina. 1997b. "The Unraveling of a Presidency." *NACLA* (May/June).

Selverston-Scher, Melina. 2000. "Ecuador Paralyzed: Indigenous Call to End Corruption." *Native Americas* (Spring).

Skocpol, Theda. 1979. *States and Social Revolutions: A Comparative Analysis of France, Russia, and China.* New York: Cambridge University Press.

Skocpol, Theda. 1982. "What Makes Peasants Revolutionary?" *Comparative Politics* (April): 351-375.

Smith, Anthony. 1971. *Theories of Nationalism.* London: Duckworth.

Smith, Anthony. 1986. *The Ethnic Origins of Nations.* London: Basil Blackwell.

Smith, Anthony. 1986. "State-making and Nation-building." In *States in History,* ed. John Hall. Oxford, U.K.: Blackwell.

Smith, Anthony. 1993. *National Identity.* Reno: University of Nevada Press.

Stavenhagen, Rodolfo. 1992. "Challenging the Nation-State in Latin America." *Journal of International Affairs* 45 (2): 421-440.

Suárez, Vinicio. 1993. Governor of Loja Province. Interview by the author.

Sylva Charvet, Paola. 1991. *La organización rural en el Ecuador*. Quito: Abya-Yala.

Taolombo, Jorge. 1993. Indigenous Affairs Office of the Prefect, Bolívar. Interview by author.

Taussig, Michael. 1990. *The Devil and Commodity Fetishism in South America*. Chapel Hill, N.C.: University of North Carolina Press.

Tilly, Charles. 1984. "Social Movements and National Politics." In *Statemaking and Social Movements*, eds. Charles Bright and Susan Harding. Ann Arbor, Mich.: University of Michigan Press.

Treakle, Kay. 1998. "Ecuador: Structural Adjustment and Indigenous and Environmental Resistance." In *The Struggle for Accountability: The World Bank, NGOs, and Grassroots Movements*, eds. Jonathan Fox and L. David Brown. Cambridge, Mass.: MIT Press.

Urban, Greg, and Joel Sherzer. 1991. *Nation-States and Indians in Latin America*. Austin, Texas: University of Texas Press.

Valarezo, Galo Ramón. 1992. "Estado plurinacional: Una propuesta innovadora atrapada en viejos conceptos." In *Pueblos Indios, Estado y Derecho*, ed. Corporación Editora Nacional. Quito: Abya-Yala.

Valarezo, Galo Ramón. 1993. *El regreso de las Runas: La potencialidad del Proyecto Indio en el Ecuador*. Quito: Comunidec.

Van Cott, Donna. 1994. *Indigenous People and Democracy in Latin America*. New York: St. Martin's Press.

Villamil, Héctor. 1993. OPIP (Organization of Indigenous Peoples of Pastaza). Interview by author.

Wade, Peter. 1997. *Race and Ethnicity in Latin America*. Chicago: Pluto Press.

Warren, Kay. 1993. *The Violence Within: Cultural and Political Opposition in Divided Nations*. Boulder, Colo.: Westview Press.

Weber, Max. 1947. *The Theory of Social and Economic Organization*. New York: Oxford University Press.

Whitehead, Lawrence. 1987. "Bolivia's Failed Democratization, 1977-1980." In *Transitions from Authoritarian Rule: Comparative Perspectives,* eds. Guillermo O'Donnell, Philippe C. Schmitter, and Laurence Whitehead. Baltimore: The Johns Hopkins University Press.

Whitten, Norman E., Jr. 1981. *Cultural Transformations and Ethnicity in Modern Ecuador*. Champaign, Ill.: University of Illinois Press.

Whitten, Norman E., Jr. 1985. *Sicuanga Runa: The Other Side of Development in Amazonian Ecuador*. Champaign, Ill.: University of Illinois Press.

Wolf, Eric. 1968. *Peasant Wars of the Twentieth Century*. New York: Harper & Row.

Yánez Cossio, Consuelo. 1991. *"Macac": Teoría y práctica de la educación indígena – Estudio de Caso en el Ecuador*. Cali, Colombia: CELATER (Centro Latinoamericano de Tecnología y Educación Rural).

Yashar, Deborah. 1997. *Indigenous Politics and Democracy: Contesting Citizenship in Latin America*. Working Paper #238 (July). Notre Dame, Ind.: University of Notre Dame, The Helen Kellogg Institute for International Studies.

Yashar, Deborah. 1999. "Democracy, Indigenous Movements, and the Post-Liberal Challenge in Latin America." *World Politics* 52 (1).

Young, Crawford. 1976. *The Politics of Cultural Pluralism*. Madison, Wis.: University of Wisconsin Press.

Young, Crawford. 1993. *The Rising Tide of Cultural Pluralism: The Nation-State at Bay?* Madison, Wis.: University of Wisconsin Press.

Zamosc, León. 1993. "Protesta agraria y movimiento indígena en la Sierra Ecuatoriana." In *Sismo étnico en el Ecuador: Varias Perspectivas*, ed. CEDIME (Centro de Investigaciones de los Movimientos Sociales del Ecuador). Quito: Abya-Yala.

Zamosc, León. 1994. "Estadística de las áreas de predominio étnico de la Sierra Ecuatoriana." Sociology Department, University of California, San Diego. Unpublished paper.

Zevallos, J. V. 1990. "Reforma agraria y cambio estructural: Ecuador Desde 1964." *Ecuador Debate* 20.

Index